RONALD MATHENY

The Cunningham Legacy

Pioneers of York County Pennsylvania

First edition

This book was professionally typeset on Reedsy.
Find out more at reedsy.com

Contents

1 Introduction 1

Our Founding Fathers a/k/a "The Begats" 1

2 John Cunningham: The Beginning of a Legacy 4

Life In York County, Pennsylvania 5

John's Early Life and Marriage to Elizabeth Spangler 6

The Home of John Cunningham 7

1860 U.S. Census for Spring Garden Township, York County, Pennsylvania: 8

From 1860 U. S. Census; Spring Garden Township, York Co., PA 10

Evidence of John Cunningham's House 17

Eli Life and Legacy 19

David Cunningham's Life and Contributions 20

Life of William Cunningham 22

William Cunningham's listing as a County Commissioner 24

The Estate of William Cunningham 25

William Cunningham's Final Last Will and Testament 25

First and Final Accounts of Executors; Albert and D.W. Cunningham 35

3 The Next Generations 48

Children of William Cunningham and Lydia Beaverson: 48
Children of Eli Cunningham and Caroline: 52
Children of David Cunningham and Kate Kohler: 55
4 Modern Era: The Cunningham Descendants 59
Children and Grandchildren of William and Almeda (Brown) Cunningham 60
5 Genealogy Resources 67
Burial Records and Cemetery Listings 74
John Cunningham and Mt. Zion Lutheran Church 74
Cornerstone 75
Grave Marker of John and Elizabeth (Spangler) Cunningham 76
John Spangler 77
John and Christina Spangler 79
Grave Marker of William Cunningham and Lydia Cunningham 81
Grave Marker of Eli and Caroline Cunningham 83
Grave Marker of the Children of Eli and Caroline Cunningham 84
Grave Marker of Walter and Lillie M. Cunningham 84
Grave Marker of John E., Alice, and Bruce R. Cunningham 85
Grave Marker of Albert Cunningham and His Wife Ida Agnes 87
Grave Marker of David and Kate Cunningham 88
Grave Marker of Charles and Emma Cunningham 89
Grave Marker of James F., Elizabeth F., and Ruth E. Cunningham 90

Grave Marker of Katie Irene Cunningham Raffensberger and Clarence E. Raffensberger 91
Grave Marker of Martin and Ethel Cunningham 92
Grave Marker of David W. and Ida J. Cunningham and Their Children 93
Cunningham Family Newspaper Announcements 95
6 Appendices 112
Legal Documents of William Cunningham Estate 112
Inventory and Appraisement Document 116
Detailed Property List Document: 123
Petition For Guardian Trust on Behalf of Elsie Cunningham 161
Guardian's Bond for Elsie Cunningham 166
Petition for Appointment of Trustee: Estate of William and Almeda Brown Cunningham 170
Trustee Granted: Estate of William and Almeda Brown Cunningham 176
Trustee Bond: Estate of William and Almeda Brown Cunningham 182
Guardian's Bond: Zachariah Myers 185
Guardian's Bond for Annie Minerva Myers 188
Guardian's Bond: Wilbur H. Myers 192
7 Acknowledgements and References 196

1

Introduction

Our Founding Fathers a/k/a "The Begats"

In the Biblical book of Genesis, there's a detailed genealogy charting Adam and Eve's descendants, pinpointing the founding fathers of humanity. A brief summation might read:

"...And Adam begat a son named Seth, and Seth begat Enos, and Enos begat Cainan, and Cainan begat Mahalaleel, and Mahalaleel begat Jared, and Jared begat Enoch, and Enoch begat Methuselah, and Methuselah begat Lamech, and Lamech begat Noah, and Noah begat Shem, Ham, and Japheth."

Biblical scholars often refer to these genealogical lines humorously as "the begats," for obvious reasons. If this method was good enough for the sacred texts to trace the spread of mankind, it's certainly apt for Springettsbury Township.

Here, we proudly present our local version of "the begats," a compendium of those founding families whose records and particulars we've managed to unearth.

Springettsbury Township is blessed to have had many distinguished individuals as the roots of our community. This book sheds light on as many as we could discover through research of our early settlers. Any omissions are purely unintentional, limited only by the available information.

Our research unveiled a tapestry of millers, blacksmiths, farmers, teachers, public officials, businesspeople, and industrious, God-fearing family men. Many readers might find the joy and excitement of tracing their lineage back to these founding families, much like some of our surviving family members have experienced. The enthusiasm grew as we compiled background information on these families, many of whom significantly contributed to the community's growth and development within our township and beyond.

Some early homesteads still stand, and some descendants of these pioneering families continue to live here, maintaining their legacy as valued community members.

It should be noted that the interweaving of family trees has led to some cross-referencing and necessary duplication of data. But in historical research, the rule of thumb is to have an abundance of information rather than too little.

The Cunningham family has a rich history rooted in York County, Pennsylvania. This genealogy book aims to preserve the legacy of the Cunningham family, celebrating their contributions and heritage through generations.

2

John Cunningham: The Beginning of a Legacy

The Journey Begins

John Cunningham: From Maryland to Pennsylvania

John Cunningham, born on January 22, 1800, in Maryland, moved to York County, Pennsylvania, at the age of 18. He initially settled in what was then Spring Garden Township, which later became Springettsbury Township. John's industrious nature led him to secure employment with George Loucks, a prominent miller and distiller. He also worked on the construction of the railroad from York to Wrightsville.

Life In York County, Pennsylvania

To provide historical context for York County during John Cunningham's lifetime, the area was a thriving agricultural region deeply rooted in the farming traditions of Pennsylvania. The early 19th century marked the height of agriculture in the state, with over 90% of its population involved in farming by 1820. York County, like much of the region, showcased the ideal Pennsylvania farm, complete with large barns, diverse crops, and livestock. The farms not only supported local economies but also symbolized the independence and prosperity of rural American life during this period.

By the mid-1800s, farming in Pennsylvania began evolving due to advancements in agricultural machinery, such as threshers and harvesters, which made farm work more efficient. This transition enabled many farmers to focus on specialized crops and products for urban markets. York County farmers, including the descendants of John Cunningham, likely contributed to this economy by diversifying their operations. Some Cunningham family members are noted for their success as orchard farmers, a key industry for York County's agricultural output, providing fruit and other produce to nearby cities.

Additionally, infrastructure developments like canals and railroads in the 19th century connected York County's agricultural products to larger markets, boosting the region's economic significance. These improvements supported businesses such as farming, milling, and other related industries.

The historical significance of John Cunningham's involvement in the founding of the Mt. Zion church highlights the family's deep ties to the community. Religious and civic leadership in such churches often intersected with economic and social contributions, further solidifying their legacy in the region.

John's Early Life and Marriage to Elizabeth Spangler

John's enterprising spirit soon turned him towards farming. He started with a small property, but through hard work and dedication, he became the owner of a 104-acre farm located two and a half miles northeast of York. With the help of his sons, he transformed the uncultivated land into a productive farm, building new structures and making significant improvements.

John played a significant role in the establishment of Mount Zion Lutheran Church and was known for his progressive and public-spirited nature. His genial disposition and kindness earned him many friends and admirers.

John Cunningham married Elizabeth Spangler, the daughter of John and Christiana (Christine) Schultz Spangler. Elizabeth was born on October 17, 1812.

The couple had eight children:

- - William
- - Susan who married William Nye
- - George and John (twins) who died at birth on July 31, 1835
- - Lucinda, born on December 30, 1840, christened on June

19, 1841, and died unmarried

- - Eli, who lived in Springettsbury Township
- - David, also of Springettsbury Township
- - Elizabeth (Mrs. Henry Schultz), who lived in the same township

John Cunningham passed away in 1866, and Elizabeth survived him until 1883.

(Adapted from "History of York County, Pennsylvania" by George Prowell)

The Home of John Cunningham

The book's cover features an image of the residence where John Cunningham and his family resided. Through a rigorous analysis of census data, land records, and other relevant documents, we have irrefutably determined the property's ownership.

Evidence of John Cunningham's House

1860 U.S. Census for Spring Garden Township, York County, Pennsylvania:

The 1860 U.S. Census provides valuable insights into the residents of what is now Springettsbury Township. This census includes individuals, their ages, professions, and the value of their real estate. The census data is crucial for understanding land ownership and the residents during that time.

- 1860 Buildings 41-50 in West Region of Springettsbury Township
- 1860 Buildings 61-70 in West Region of Springettsbury Township
- 1860 Buildings 71-80 in West Region of Springettsbury Township

Shown on 1860 Map of York County contains the owner/occupant of most buildings; for example (w57) is J. Oaks. Additional information on J. Oaks can be found by consulting the 1860 Census of the United States; where one discovers this is John Oaks, a 50-year-old, millwright, with $1,200 in real estate holdings.

The results after consulting 1860 Spring Garden Township census records are shown below. Spring Garden Township 1860 Census records must be used because Springettsbury Township was formed from the northeast part of that township on April 20, 1891. The order of visitation, of the census taker, often provides assistance on who are neighbors and the tabulation of "value of real estate" separates the landowners from the renters or tenants:

Census for Land which is now Springettsbury Township
From 1860 U. S. Census; Spring Garden Township, York Co., PA

[w59]

Number (Assigned on 1860 Map)	Families—numbered in Order of Visitation	Surname	Given Name	Age (as of June 1, 1860)	Profession	Value of Real Estate
w51	15	Diehl	Jacob	27	Farmer	(A)
w52	12	Baish	John	43	Farmer	(A)
[w53]	6	Strabbe	Herman	42	Laborer	(A)
w54	5	Loucks	Henry	28	Farmer	$20,000
[w55]	26	Gipe	Peter (B)	73	Farmer	$1,600
w56	30	Billet	Samuel	48	Laborer	(A)
w57	28	Oaks	John	50	Millwright	$1,200
w58	13	Walker	Joseph	23	Carpenter	(A)
[w59]	27	Cunningham	John (C)	60 *	Farmer	$7,250
w60	16	Fischer	Jonathan	37	Farmer	(C)

[Still Standing] * age=60 in 1860; per age=50 record in 1850 Census

(A) Five marked 1860 sites are not identified; these are likely "renters"

(B) Jacob Walk originally thought to reside [w46]; reconsider w/[w55]

(C) John Cunningham owns [w: 59, 19, 20 & 60]; assume last 3 rented

Two mapped 1860 buildings, [w57] and [w58], warrant further evaluation, as far as their 1860 status. **Three of the mapped 1860 buildings likely still stand at these addresses:**

- [w53] – 500 Paradise Road
- [w55] – 2209 North Sherman Street
- [w59] – 1211 Druck Valley Road

In the 1860 Census, house number 26 [w55 on the 1860 Map] is recorded as having two families residing therein; family number 26 is the family of Peter Gipe, and family number 25 is the family of Jacob Walker. Walker was originally thought to reside at [w46], per a previous post in this series; a correction will be made per this Census observation.

[w59] Residence of John Cunningham (1800-1866)

John Cunningham was born in Maryland in 1800 and settled in York County, Pennsylvania during 1818. **George Prowell's 1907 *History of York County, PA* describes John Cunningham's early life on pages 407-408 of Volume II; quoting:**

Census for Land which is now Springettsbury Township

From 1860 U. S. Census; Spring Garden Township, York Co., PA

| Number (Assigned on 1860 Map) | Families numbered in Order of Visitation | Name | Age (as of June 1, 1860) | Profession | Value of Real Estate

- | W51 | 12 | Diehl, Jacob | 27 | Farmer | {A} |
- | W52 | 18 | Isiah, John | 13 | Farmer | {A} |
- | W53 | 6 | Staabie, Heyman | 42 | Laborer | {A} |
- | W54 | 10 | Loucks, Henry | 28 | Farmer | $20,000 |
- | W55 | 26 | Gipe, Peter | 73 | Farmer | $1,600 |
- | in30 | Billett, Samuel | 48 | Laborer | {A} |
- | W57 | 8 | Oaks, John | 50 | Millwright | $1,200 |
- | W58 | 13 | Walker, Joseph | 23 | Carpenter | {A} |
- | W59 | 17 | Cunningham, John | 60 | Farmer | $7,250 |
- | W60 | 16 | Fiedler, Jonathan | 37 | Farmer | {C} |

[Still Standing] *age=60 in 1860; per age=50 record in 1850 Census

{A} Five marked 1860 sites are not identified; these are likely "renters"

{B} Jacob Walk originally thought to reside [w46]; reconsider w[W55]

{C} John Cunningham owns [w: 59, 19, 20 & 60]; assume last 3 rented

Residences and Properties Noted in the 1860 Census:

- [W53] – 500 Paradise Road
- [W57] – 2209 North Sherman Street**
- [W59] – 1211 Druck Valley Road, John Cunningham's Residence:
- [W59] Residence of John Cunningham (1800-1866)

He came from his native State [Maryland] to York County {Pennsylvania] at the age of eighteen and settled near York in the present area of Springettsbury Township. He first secured employment with George Loucks, a prominent miller and distiller, and also assisted in the construction of the railroad from York to Wrightsville [completed in 1840].

Being active and enterprising, he turned his attention to farming. He first purchased a small property. By diligence and attentiveness to duty he became the owner of a farm containing 104 acres, two and a half miles northeast of York. When John Cunningham purchased this land most of it was uncultivated. By the assistance of his sons, he cleared the land and made it rich and productive, erected new farm buildings, made many other improvements, and pursued farming as his occupation the remainder of his life.

Shearer's 1860 Map of York County show "J. Cunningham" identified on four dwellings, centering near the western end of Druck Valley Road. Two of these dwelling [w59] and [w60] are on the north side of Druck Valley Road, while dwellings [w19] and [w20] are on the south side of the road; their location placement on the map does allow all these dwellings to fit within a 104-acre footprint.
The 1860 Census listing for John Cunningham records all his children still living in his household; except for his eldest son William, a Master Carpenter, living at [w42] along North Sherman Street. Thus it is likely that three of John's four dwellings were being rented out to tenants.

Which of the four dwellings was the John Cunningham residence?
In the 1880 United States Census, the widow Elizabeth Cunningham resides in the same dwelling as the family of her daughter Elizabeth; i.e. family of Henry and Elizabeth Schultz. John Cunningham died in 1866. His wife Elizabeth (Spangler) Cunningham lived until 1883.

Beach Nichols' 1876 Atlas of York County provided the clue. The neighbors to Elizabeth Cunningham, per the 1880 Census are consistent with 1876 map neighbors per [w59] location. On the 1876 map, the dwelling at the [w59] location is marked "Mrs. Cunningham." There is no dwelling at the [w60] location. Also on the 1876 map, the families of two of John's sons reside in the dwellings on the south side of Druck Valley Road. Eli Cunningham resides in [w19] and David Cunningham resides in [w20]. **In all likelihood, John Cunningham (1800-1866), with his wife and five children, lived in the following dwelling at least from 1860 and onward.**

Shearer's 1860 Map of York County shows "J. Cunningham" identified on four dwellings, centering near the western end of Druck Valley Road. Two of these dwellings ([W59] and [W60]) are on the north side of Druck Valley Road, while dwellings ([W19] and [W20]) are on the south side of the road; their location placement on the map does allow all these dwellings to fit within a 104-acre footprint.

The 1860 Census listing for John Cunningham records all his children still living in his household; except for his eldest son William, a Master Carpenter, living at [W42] along North Sherman Street. Thus, it is likely that three of John's four dwellings were being rented out to tenants.

Which of the four dwellings was the John Cunningham residence?

In the 1880 United States Census, the widow Elizabeth Cunningham resides in the same dwelling as the family of her daughter Elizabeth (family of Henry and Elizabeth Schultz). John Cunningham died in 1866. His wife Elizabeth (Spangler) Cunningham lived until 1883.

Beach Nichols' 1876 Atlas of York County provided the clue. The neighbors to Elizabeth Cunningham, per the 1880 Census, are consistent with 1876 map neighbors per [W59] location. On the 1876 map, the dwelling at the [W59] location is marked "Mrs. Cunningham." There is no dwelling at the [W60] location. Also on the 1876 map, the families of two of John's sons reside in the dwellings on the south side of Druck Valley Road. Eli Cunningham resides in [W19] and David Cunningham resides in [W20]. In all likelihood, John Cunningham (1800-1866), with his wife and five children, lived in the following dwelling at least from 1860 and onward.

Visuals for Reference

1860 Buildings and 1937 Aerial Photo:

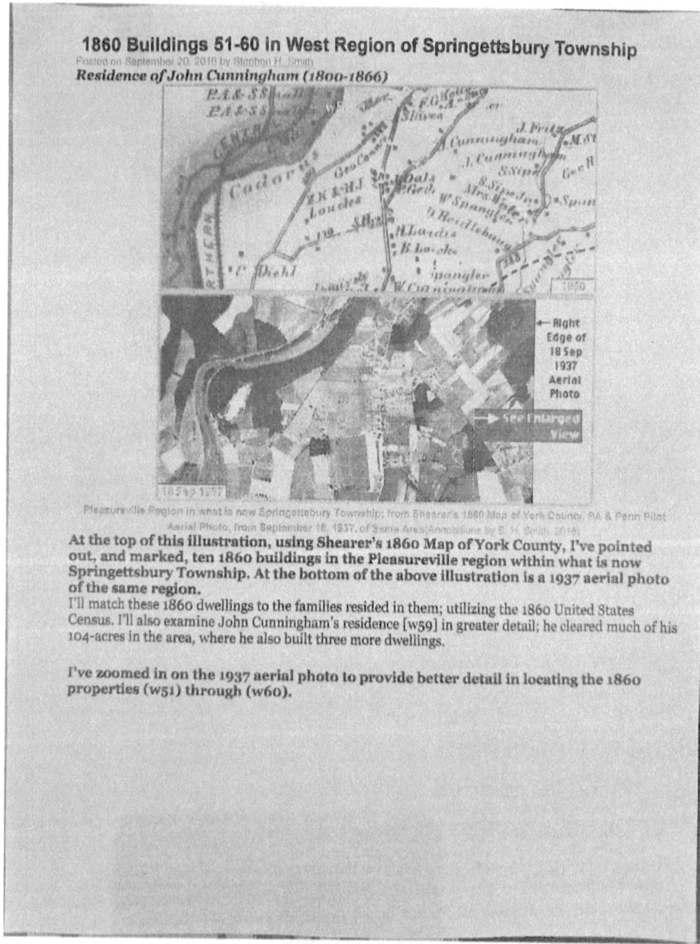
1860 Buildings 51-60 in West Region of Springettsbury Township

Posted on September 20, 2016 by Stephen H. Smith

Residence of John Cunningham (1800-1866)

Pleasureville Region in what is now Springettsbury Township; from Shearer's 1860 Map of York County, PA & Penn Pilot Aerial Photo, from September 18, 1937, of Same Area(Annotations by S. H. Smith, 2016)

At the top of this illustration, using Shearer's 1860 Map of York County, I've pointed out, and marked, ten 1860 buildings in the Pleasureville region within what is now Springettsbury Township. At the bottom of the above illustration is a 1937 aerial photo of the same region.

I'll match these 1860 dwellings to the families resided in them; utilizing the 1860 United States Census. I'll also examine John Cunningham's residence [w59] in greater detail; he cleared much of his 104-acres in the area, where he also built three more dwellings.

I've zoomed in on the 1937 aerial photo to provide better detail in locating the 1860 properties (w51) through (w60).

Enlarged View of Penn Pilot Aerial Photo, from September 18, 1937, in Pleasureville region within Springettsbury Township (Annotations by S. H. Smith, 2016)

I'm working my way around Springettsbury Township until all buildings from 1860 are visited. See the post: for my specification of the four regions. With this post, I've completed an examination of the property owners for all 1860 buildings in the North, East and South regions of Springettsbury Township. Three more posts will complete this series; they will focus on the Pleasureville area in the West region.
Links to other posts in this series include:

As a side note, when properties (w1) through (w10) were first visited, the precise 1860 owners of only two of the properties could be identified. Initial deed searches have now increased that number to seven. 1860 owners of properties (w1) through (w10) will be posted upon the discovery of the final th

Enlarged View of Penn Pilot Aerial Photo, from September 18, 1937, in Pleasureville region within Springettsbury Township (Annotations by S. H. Smith, 2016)

I'm working my way around Springettsbury Township until all

buildings from 1860 are visited. See the post: Springettsbury Township building tally during 1860, for my specification of the four regions. With this post, I've completed an examination of the property owners for all 1860 buildings in the North, East, and South regions of Springettsbury Township. Three more posts will complete this series; they will focus on the Pleasureville area in the West region. Links to other posts in this series include:

- - 1860 Buildings 1-10 in North Region of Springettsbury Township
- - 1860 Buildings 11-20 in North Region of Springettsbury Township
- - 1860 Buildings 21-24 in North Region of Springettsbury Township
- - 1860 Buildings 25-31 in North Region of Springettsbury Township
- - 1860 Buildings 32-35 in North Region of Springettsbury Township
- - 1860 Buildings 1-10 in South Region of Springettsbury Township
- - 1860 Buildings 11-20 in South Region of Springettsbury Township
- - 1860 Buildings 21-31 in South Region of Springettsbury Township
- - 1860 Buildings 31-35 in South Region of Springettsbury Township
- - 1860 Buildings 36-41 in South Region of Springettsbury Township
- - 1860 Buildings 1-10 in East Region of Springettsbury

Township

- - 1860 Buildings 11-20 in East Region of Springettsbury Township
- - 1860 Buildings 21-30 in East Region of Springettsbury Township
- - 1860 Buildings 31-40 in East Region of Springettsbury Township
- - 1860 Buildings 41-58 in East Region of Springettsbury Township
- - 1860 Buildings 1-10 in West Region of Springettsbury Township
- - 1860 Buildings 11-20 in West Region of Springettsbury Township
- - 1860 Buildings 21-30 in West Region of Springettsbury Township

Evidence of John Cunningham's House

Dwelling at 1211 Druck Valley Road, Springettsbury Township, York County, PA (2012 Photo)

This detailed look at the John Cunningham residence [W59] will result in a required correction to [W19]; i.e., the removal of John Cunningham and replacing with the nearest available renter per Census visitation order. I've also added another example to my list of Census Record Oddities. The 1850 Census notes John Cunningham is 50 years old; agreeing with church records and his gravestone at Mt. Zion Cemetery. The 1860 Census incorrectly notes John Cunningham is 48 years old; which was initially misleading when doing family history research on

John.

Dwelling at 1211 Druck Valley Road, Springettsbury Township, York County, PA (2012 Photo)

This detailed look at the John Cunningham residence [w59] will result in a required correction to ; i.e. the remove of John Cunningham and replacing with the nearest available renter per Census visitation order. **I've also added another example to my list of Census Record Oddities.** The 1850 Census notes John Cunningham is 50-years-old; agreeing with church records and his gravestone at Mt. Zion Cemetery. The 1860 Census incorrectly notes John Cunningham is 48-years-old; which was initially misleading when doing family history research on John.

About Stephen H. Smith

Stephen H. Smith is a design engineer who worked at York International Corp. for 33 years before retiring several years ago to research and write books full time; his second career. The initial emphasis was on family history when he won a national award during 2002 for his first book "Barshingers in America." Positive feedback and that award were influential in his decision to retire early from engineering and start a retirement career.

This entry was posted in all posts, Buildings, Family Histories, Maps, Pennsylvania, Roads, York County and tagged 1211 Druck Valley Road, 1860 Map of York County PA, 1860 United States Census, 1937 Penn Pilot Aerial Photo, 2209 North Sherman Street, 920 Paradise Road, Beach Nichols 1876 Atlas of York County PA, Census Record Oddities, Codorus Creek, David Cunningham, Druck Valley Road, Eden Road, Eli Cunningham, Elizabeth Cunningham, Elizabeth Spangler, George Loucks, George Prowell's 1907 History of York County PA, Henry Loucks, Henry Schultz, Harman Strabba, Jacob Diehl, John Baish, John Cunningham, John Cunningham (1800-1866), John Oaks, Jonathan Fiedler, Joseph Walker, Maryland, Master Carpenter, Millwright, Mrs. Cunningham, Mt. Zion Cemetery, North Sherman Street, Paradise Road, Peter Gipe, Pleasureville PA, Railroad from York to Wrightsville, Ridgewood Road, Samuel Ellis, Shearer's 1860 Map of York County PA, Spring Garden Township 1860 Census, Spring Garden Township PA, Springettsbury Township PA, William Cunningham, Wrightsville PA. Bookmark the permalink.

About Stephen H. Smith

Stephen H. Smith is a design engineer who worked at York International Corp. for 33 years before retiring several years ago to research and write books full-time; his second career. The initial emphasis was on family history when he won a national award during 2002 for his first book "Barshingers in America." Positive feedback and that award were influential in his decision to retire early from engineering and start a retirement career.

Eli Life and Legacy

Eli Cunningham grew up on his father John Cunningham's farm, spending his childhood working the land and attending public school during the winter months. His dedication to farming continued into adulthood, and he eventually took over part of the family homestead. Eli not only managed the farm but also developed a deep interest in fruit cultivation, successfully raising large quantities of apples and peaches.

In 1893, Eli retired from active farming, passing the responsibility to his son. His achievements in agriculture were complemented by his active role in the community and local politics. Eli was a devoted Democrat and frequently represented his party in county conventions and committee meetings. He served as an assessor, road surveyor, and held various other offices in his township. In December 1894, he was appointed as the mercantile appraiser for York County, a position he held for one term.

Eli's community involvement extended to his religious life. He was a committed Lutheran and served as an elder at Mount Zion

Church, a congregation his father helped establish.

In the spring of 1867, Eli married Caroline Loucks, the daughter of Jacob and Leah (Rudy) Loucks. Together, they had several children:

- - John E.: Managed his father's farm, married Alice Christ, and had four children: Bruce, Mallie, Eli, and an infant named Emma.
- - Emma: Married Henry Leckrone, a farmer in Springettsbury, and had seven children: George Elias, Morris William, Carrie May, Allen Howard, Anthony Jacob, Walter Dewey, and Paul Raymond.
- - Walter: A painter by trade, married Lillie Snyder, and had one child, Ray.
- - Dora: Married George Worley, lived at home with their parents, and had two children: Grace and Stewart.

Eli's life was marked by his dedication to farming, his active participation in the community, and his leadership within his church.

David Cunningham's Life and Contributions

David Cunningham, born on October 12, 1839, in Springettsbury Township, was the second son of John and Elizabeth (Spangler) Cunningham. David received his education in public schools but began working on his father's farm from a young age.

As he grew older, he chose to dedicate his life to farming, eventually owning 67 acres of the family homestead and two residential properties. Known for his energy and business acumen, David cultivated a peach orchard with 400 trees and became a successful farmer and businessman.

David was a steadfast Democrat and actively participated in local politics, always striving to contribute to the public welfare. He married Kate Kohler, the daughter of Henry and Mary (Cramer) Kohler, on February 26, 1869. Together, they had eight children, each contributing to the family's legacy:

- 1. Elmira C. (Mrs. Samuel Hess): Lived in York Township.
- 2. Charles: Worked as the yard boss at the York freight depot of the Pennsylvania Railroad, married Emma Stough of Springettsbury Township.
- 3. James: A molder by profession, married Lizzie Sheugh-berger of Lancaster, PA.
- 4. Nettie (Mrs. Henry Moul): Resided in Eberton.
- 5. Luther: Married Emma Boyer of Eberton.
- 6. Susan: Taught school for seven years before marrying Edward Heikes of Manchester Township.
- 7. George
- 8. William

The Cunningham family was deeply connected to the Lutheran Church, where David served as an elder, reflecting his strong community ties and religious faith.

Life of William Cunningham

William Cunningham, the son of John Cunningham, was a prominent figure in York County as a Master Carpenter by trade. Born in August 1832, William married Lydia A., who was born on May 12, 1832. Together, they raised several children and contributed to the family legacy in Springettsbury Township.

In the 1850 census, William is listed as an 18-year-old laborer living in the household of John Spangler in Spring Garden Township. By the 1880 census, he is recorded as residing in Spring Garden Township with his wife Lydia and their children: John (17), David (13), Elizabeth (9), and Anna C. (9).

William's Probate and Descendants

William Cunningham passed away on July 25, 1899. His probate records indicate that Albert and David W. Cunningham served as executors. His surviving children included Albert, David W., Ellen (Mrs. Horace Myers), and others.

Lydia A., William's wife, passed away on October 10, 1894. The couple is buried at Mt. Zion Lutheran Church Cemetery in Springettsbury Township, along with several of their descendants.

William Cunningham (Ex-County Commissioner of York County, PA)

- (B): August 4, 1832
- (D): July 25, 1899
- Wife: Lydia Beaverson

- (B): May 12, 1832
- (D): December 10, 1900
- Father: Mr. Beaverson
- Mother: Unknown
- **Notes**: Master Carpenter by trade; County Commissioner for 3 years (1894-1896)
- They had 7 children:

Ellen who married Horace D. Myers

Albert

William

John P.

David W.

Elizabeth B.

Anna Catherine

William Cunningham's listing as a County Commissioner

ments. There is therefore no record of these deputies in this county, but among them were George A. Barnitz and William H. Kurtz, just previous to 1850. The following is a list of the district attorneys of York County after the office was made elective, together with the dates of their election:

James E. Buchanan, 1850; Thomas A. Ziegle, appointed, 1851; Richard P. Wilton, elected, 1853; William C. Chapman, 1856; John W. Bittenger, 1862; David J. Williams, 1868; Arthur N. Green, 1871; John Blackford, 1874; John W. Heller, 1877; Edward D. Ziegler, 1880; George W. McElroy, 1883; N. M. Wanner, 1886; Edward D. Bentzel, 1889; William A. Miller, 1892; Joseph R. Strawbridge, 1895; William B. Gemmill, 1898; Allen C. Wiest, 1901; James G. Glessner, 1904.

County Commissioners. The office of county commissioner in York County has always been elective. At the first election held there were three commissioners chosen, who were divided into three classes, one of them to serve one year, one to serve two years, and one three years. From 1749 to 1875, one commissioner was elected annually to serve for three years. The new constitution of 1873 provided for the election of three commissioners in 1875, and every third year the same number thereafter. This constitution also provides that the political party in the minority should be entitled to one member of the board of commissioners.

FIRST CLASS.

1749—George Schwaabe.
1751—Bartholomew Maul.
1754—Peter Shugard.
1757—Martin Eichelberger.
1760—James Welsch.
1763—William Douglass.
1766—Joseph Updegraff.
1769—John Heckendorn.
1772—John Hay.
1775—Michael Hahn.
1776—William Ross.
1777—William Ross.
1778—Philip Rothrock.
1781—Jacob Schmeiser.
1784—Michael Hahn.
1787—Godfrey Lenhart.
1790—John Spengler.
1793—Joseph Welshans.
1796—John Forsythe.
1799—Daniel Spangler.
1802—Christopher Lauman.
1805—Abraham Graffius.
1808—Jacob Heckert.
1811—Peter Small.
1814—Jacob Spangler.
1817—John Barnitz.
1820—Michael Doudel.
1823—Henry Schmeiser.
1826—John Voglesong.
1829—Peter Ahl.
1832—Jacob Dietz.

SECOND CLASS.

1749—Walter Sharp.
1750—William McClellan.
1752—John Mikel.
1755—Thomas McCartney.
1758—William Delap.
1761—George Myers.
1764—Philip Ziegler.
1767—Hugh Dunwoodie.
1770—John Monteith.
1773—Henry Tyson.
1776—John Hay.
1779—John Sample.
1782—William Cochran.
1785—Robert Morrison.
1786—William McClellan.
1791—John Morrow.
1794—Henry Welsh.
1797—John Edie.
1800—Anthony Hinkle.
1803—Robert Ramsey.
1806—Christopher Hetrick.
1809—Frederick Hoke.
1812—John Kauffelt.
1815—Joseph Reed.
1818—Andrew Ketterman.
1821—Michael Newman.
1824—Mathew Clark.
1827—Philip Henise.
1830—William Patterson.
1833—John Shultz.

THIRD CLASS.

1749—Patrick Watson.
1753—James Agnew.
1756—Robert McPherson.
1758—John Frankelberger.
1759—John Adlum.
1762—Samuel Edie.
1765—Thomas Stockton.
1768—William Gemmill.
1792—William Nelson.
1795—James Black.
1798—James McCandless.
1801—Samuel Nelson.
1802—Jacob Heckert.
1804—Jacob Glancy.
1807—William Collins.
1810—John Klein.
1813—Peter Reider.
1816—Charles Emig.
1819—Stephen T. Cooper.
1822—Peter Wolfhart.
1825—Charles Diehl.
1828—Daniel Kimmel.
1831—John W. Hetrick.
1833—Samuel Harnish.

The date of the election is given in the following list:

1836—John Beck.
1837—William Nicholas.
1838—John Reiman.
1839—Jacob Newman.
1840—David Maish.
1841—Henry Logan.
1842—Valentine B. Wentz.
1843—Thomas Kerr.
1844—Joseph Detweiler.
1845—George Eichelberger.
1846—Daniel Ginder.
1847—John Emig.
1849—John Moore.
1850—David Leber.
1851—Philip Sheffer.
1852—George Dick.
1853—Felix C. Herbert.
1854—John Myers.
1855—Aaron G. Blackford.
1856—Jesse Workinger.
1857—Daniel Meisenhelder.
1858—Jacob Greenfield.
1859—Adam Paules.
1860—Adam H. Smith.
1861—John Hyde.
1862—Henry Miller.
1863—John E. Anstine.
1864—William Reeser.
1865—Henry Hammond.
1866—Daniel Miller.
1867—William Wintermoyer.
1868—R. Duncan Brown.
1869—Peter Strickhouser.
1870—Lewis Strayer.
1871—Jacob Kohler.
1872—David Smyser.
1873—Jacob Knisely.
1874—N. E. Leber.
1875—Thomas Platt.
1875—John Pfaltzgraff.
1878—John Beard.
1878—Jacob Lamotte.
1878—J. Klinedinst.
1881—Stephen Keefer.
1881—Charles Haines.
1881—Jacob S. Bentz.
1884—George Anthony.
1884—Henry Anstine.
1884—John F. Beck.
1887—Washington H. McCreary.
1887—William Barton.
1887—Robert J. Belt.
1890—Thomas Julius.
1890—George Wise.
1890—Israel F. Gross.
1893—William Cunningham.
1893—Alewese Gruver.
1893—Jacob Leitheiser.
1896—George W. Atticks.
1896—A. K. Straley.
1896—R. S. McDonald.
1899—John Miller (died in office).
1899—Jeremiah Z. Hildebrand.
1899—Freizer Altland.
1899—Eli H. Zeigler.
1902—Jeremiah Z. Hildebrand.
1902—George F. Bortner.
1902—H. Kister Free.
1905—George W. Holtzinger.
1905—Robert G. Kessler.
1905—Emanuel Hartman.

COUNTY BUILDINGS.

An act of the General Assembly passe[d] August 19, 1749, named Thomas Co[x], Michael Tanner, George Swope, Natha[n] Hussey, and John Wright, Jr., as commis[-] sioners to carry out its provisions in for[m]

Adapted from "History of York County, Pennsylvania" by George Prowell

The Estate of William Cunningham

"This introduction outlines the initial legal proceedings for the Cunningham estate. More detailed legal documents, including asset distribution, guardianship petitions, and individual wills, are provided in the subsequent chapter, '**Legal Documents of the William Cunningham Estate**'."

William Cunningham's Final Last Will and Testament

William Cunningham must have known of his imminent death as he wrote his last will and testament on May 15, 1899, two months before his death. The following pages will be transcribed and summarized from the handwritten documents.

Front Cover:

The document is the cover sheet of the last will and testament of William Cunningham, dated July 28, 1899. It includes handwritten details such as his name, location (Springettsbury Township, York County, Pennsylvania), and the recording information (Will Book No. 14, page 266).

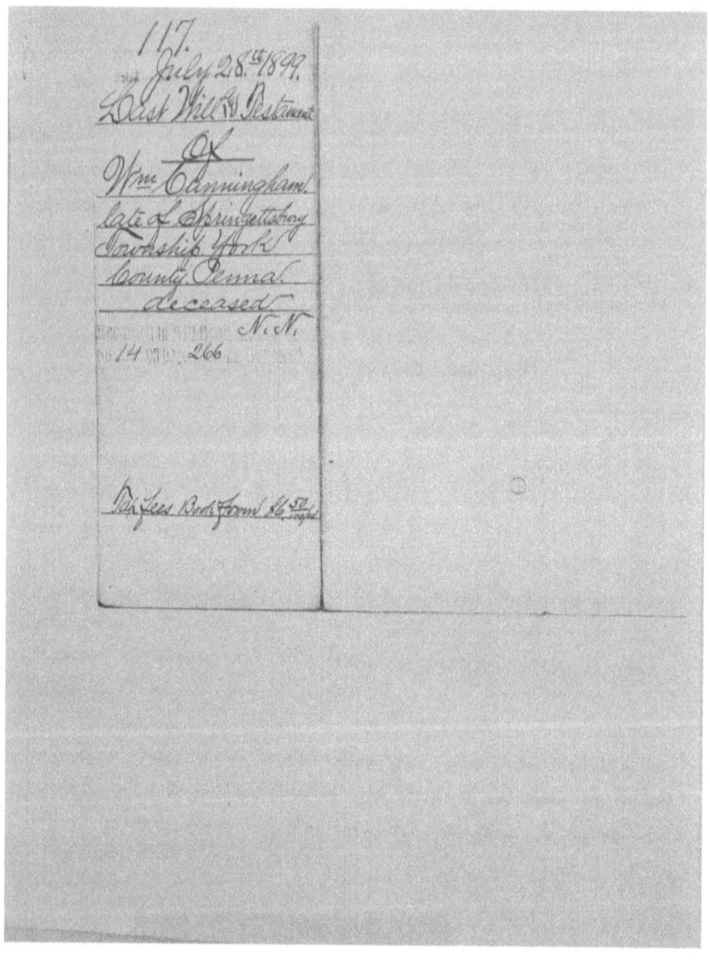

117.
July 28th 1899.
Last Will & Testament
Of
Wm Cunningham
late of L. Springettsbury
Township York
County Penna.
deceased
N.N.
14 266

Tax fees Book form $6.50

Page 1:

The first page of the document is the beginning of William Cunningham's last will and testament. It is written in cursive and details the distribution of his estate. Here is a transcription of the text:

In the name of God amen. I, William Cunningham of the Township of Springetts in the County of York, State of Pennsylvania, being of sound mind and memory, do make, publish and declare this my last will and testament in manner following (that is to say):

I order that all my just debts, funeral expenses, and charge of proving this my will be in the first place fully paid and satisfied, and after payment thereof and expenses of settling my estate and every part thereof, I make the following bequests:

First: I bequeath to my son Albert Cunningham the piece of ground on which is erected a house known as the Ferree property to be his absolutely in fee simple.

Second: I bequeath to my son David W. Cunningham the piece of ground on which is erected a house known as the Wallick property to be his absolutely in fee simple.

Third: I order and direct that all the remainder of my property, real and personal, whatsoever I am possessed of, be put up at public sale and sold to the highest and best bidder.

In the Name of God amen. I William Cunningham
of the Twp of Springetts in the County of York
State of Pennsylvania. being of sound mind and
memory. do make publish and declare this my
last will and testament in manner following
(that is to say) I order that all my just debts
funeral expenses and charge of proving this
my will be in the first place fully paid
and satisfied and after payment thereof and
expenses of settling my estate and every part
thereof I make the following bequeath

First I bequeath to my son Albert Cunningham
The piece of ground on which is erected a house
known as the Renee property to be his absolutely
in fee simple.

Second I bequeath to my son David H. Cunningham
The piece of ground on which is erected a
house known as the Wallick property to be his
Absolutely in fee simple

Third I order and direct that all the remainder of my
property real & personal of whatever I am possessed
to be put up at public sale and sole to the
highest and best bidder.

Page 2:

The share coming to my son John Cunningham I bequeath to his daughter Elsie Cunningham when she comes of age 21 years.

Until then, it shall be put on interest, and the interest shall be paid to my son John for the support of his said daughter Elsie Cunningham.

The share coming to my son William Cunningham I bequeath the half to his first wife Almeda Cunningham (formerly Brown). She shall have the interest of it only as long as she lives. After her death, it shall go to her son Harry Cunningham. The other half shall go to my son William Cunningham.

The share of my daughter Mrs. Harris (sic Horace) Myers née Ellen Cunningham shall be equally divided among her children, share and share alike, except Charles H. Myers, who shall only have twenty dollars out of his share. The balance of his coming to him shall go to his sister Annie Minerva Myers.

I bequeath to Albert Cunningham an equal share in addition to the herein bequeathed property.

I bequeath to David W. Cunningham an equal share in addition to the herein bequeathed property.

The Share comming to My Son John Cunningham I bequeth to his Daughter Elsie Cunningham when she becomes of age 21 yrs until then it shall be put on intrest and the intrest shall be paid to my Son John for the support of his said Daughter Elsie Cunningham.

The share comming to my son William Cunningham I bequeth the half to his first wife Almeda Cunningham Brown she to have the Intrest of it only so long as she lives after her death it shall ~~go to her Son Harry Cunningham~~ the other half shall go to my son William Cunningham

The Share of My Daughter Mrs Harris Myers ne' Ellen Cunningham shall be equally divided among her children share & share alike except Charles H Myers who shall only have twenty dollars out of his share. the balance of his share comming to him shall go to his sister Annie Minnie Myers.

I bequeth to Albert Cunningham an equal share in addition to the herein bequeth property

I bequeth to David W Cunningham an equal share in Addition to the herein bequeth property

Page 3:

I hereby constitute and appoint my two sons, Albert Cunningham and David W. Cunningham, my executors of this my last will and testament. I hereby give full power and authority to all my real estate not herein specifically devised and to grant and make such full and complete deeds therefor as I might if living.

In witness whereof, I, the said testator, have to this my last will and testament set my hand and seal this 15 day of May A.D. 1899.

Witnesses:
J.B. Heindel
J.G. Myers

Wm. Cunningham (seal)

I hereby constitute and appoint my two sons Albert Cunningham and David G Cunningham my executors of this my last will and testament. I hereby give full power and authority to sell all my real estate not herein specifically devised and to grant and make such full and complete deeds therefor as I might if living.

In witness whereof I the said testator have to this my last will and testament set my hand and seal this 15 day of May A D 1849.

Witness. Wm Cunningham (Seal)
J.B. Heindel
J G Myers.

Final page:

York County, ss:

Before me, Philip J. Barnhart, Register for the Probate of Wills and for granting Letters Testamentary and of Administration, in and for said County, personally appeared J.B. Heindel and J.G. Myers, the subscribing witnesses to the foregoing Last Will and Testament, who, upon being duly qualified according to law, do depose and say that they were personally present and saw and heard Wm. Cunningham, the testator, late of Springettsbury

Township, York County, Pennsylvania, deceased, the testator sign, seal, publish, pronounce and declare the within and foregoing instrument of writing as and for his Last Will and Testament, and at the time of so doing the testator was of sound and disposing mind, memory and understanding, to the best of their knowledge and belief, and that they witnessed the same at the request of the testator and in his presence and in the presence of each other at the same time.

Approved and subscribed to before me this 28th day of July A.D., 1899

Philip J. Barnhart, Register of Wills.

July 28th, A.D., 1899, the above Last Will and Testament of Wm. Cunningham, deceased, is duly admitted to probate.

Philip J. Barnhart, Register of Wills.

MEMORANDUM.

Wm. Cunningham, the said decedent, died on the 25th day of July, A.D., 1899, at or about the hour of 4:30 o'clock P.M., of said day, as per affidavit of death in Book No. 10, page 51, filed on the 28th day of July, A.D., 1899.

Letters Testamentary on the foregoing Will of Wm. Cunningham, deceased, were granted to Albert Cunningham and David W. Cunningham, the Executors named in the said Will, after being duly qualified according to law, on the 28th day of July, A.D., 1899.

Philip J. Barnhart, Register of Wills.

No. 117. Filed July 28th, A.D., 1899.

York County, ss:

Before me, Philip J. Barnhart, Register for the Probate of Wills and for granting Letters Testamentary and of Administration, in and for said County, personally appeared J. B. Heindel and Dr. J. C. Myers the subscribing witnesses to the foregoing Last Will and Testament, who, upon being duly qualified according to law, do depose and say that they were personally present and saw and heard Wm Cunningham late of Springettsbury Township, York County, Pennsylvania, deceased, the testator, sign, seal, publish, pronounce and declare the within and foregoing instrument of writing as and for his Last Will and Testament, and at the time of his so doing he the testator was of sound and disposing mind, memory and understanding, to the best of their knowledge and belief, and that they witnessed the same at the request of the testator and in his presence and in the presence of each other at the same time.

Affirmed and subscribed to before me the 28th day of July, A. D., 1899.
Philip J. Barnhart, Register of Wills.

J. B. Heindel
J. C. Myers

And now, to wit: July 28th A. D., 1899, the above Last Will and Testament of Wm Cunningham deceased, is duly admitted to probate.
Philip J. Barnhart, Register of Wills.

MEMORANDUM.

Wm Cunningham the said decedent, died on the 25th day of July A. D., 1899, at or about the hour of 4:30 o'clock, P. M., of said day, as per affidavit of death in Book No. 10, page 51, filed on the 28th day of July A. D., 1899.

Letters Testamentary on the foregoing Will of Wm Cunningham deceased, were granted to Albert Cunningham and David W. Cunningham the Executors named in the said Will, after being duly qualified according to law, on the 28th day of July A. D., 1899.

Philip J. Barnhart Register of Wills.

No. 117. Filed July 28th A. D., 1899.

Renunciation of

First and Final Accounts of Executors; Albert and D.W. Cunningham

The five-page document appears to detail the financial accounts related to the estate of William Cunningham, dated October 31, 1901. The document includes handwritten entries and some typed text, detailing various financial transactions. It mentions Albert Cunningham and D. W. Cunningham as executors of William Cunningham's estate, with signatures from relevant parties, including A. N. Green, Attorney.

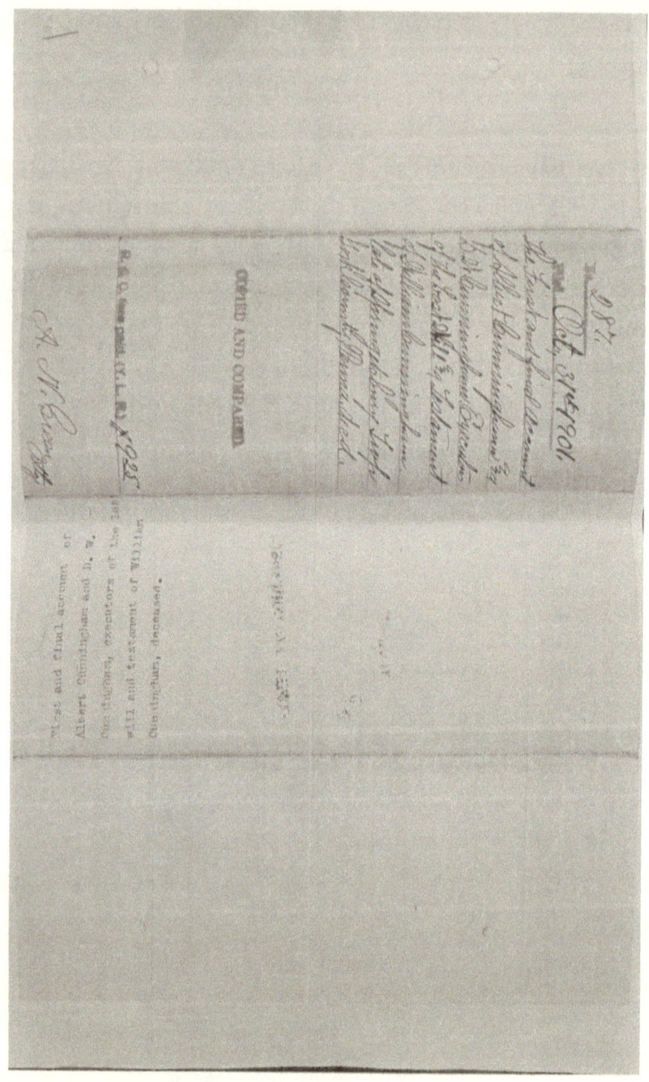

COPIED AND COMPARED

First and final account of
Albert Cunningham and D. W.
Cunningham, executors of the last
will and testament of William
Cunningham, deceased.

The first and final account of Albert Cunningham and D.W. Cunningham, executors of the last will and testament of William Cunningham, late Springettsbury Township, York County, Pennsylvania.

Dr.

- The accountants charge themselves with the amount of inventory and appraisement filed in the Register's Office, of York County, amounting to $672.40
- With amount received from Pleasureville Relief Asso. $62.00
- With amount received for willows $4.00
- With amount received for pears $0.50
- With amount received for tobacco $6.34
- With amount received for rent $20.00
- With amount received for rent $14.00
- With amount received for rent $8.00
- With interest $2.50
- With amount received for marketing $2.63
- With amount received for rent $100.00
- With interest $2.50
- With amount received for laths $5.25
- From the sale of the real estate: tract No. 1 $2525.00, tract No. 2 $180.00, with interest $37.89

The first and final account of Albert Cunningham and D. W. Cunningham, executors of the last will and testament of William Cunningham, late of Springetsbury Township, York County, Pennsylvania.

Dr.

The accountants charge themselves with the amount of inventory and appraisement filed in the Register's Office, of York County, amounting to $ 672.40

With amount received from Pleasureville Relief Asso.				62.00
"	"	"	for willows	4.00
"	"	"	for pears	.50
"	"	"	for tobacco	60.34
"	"	"	for rent	20.00
"	"	"	for rent	14.00
"	"	"	for rent	6.00
"	"	"	being interest	2.50
"	"	"	for marketing	2.63
"	"	"	for rent	100.00
"	"	"	being interest	2.80
"	"	"	for laths	5.25
"	"	"	from the sale of the real estate tract No. 1	2635.00
			tract No. 2	180.00
"	"	"	being interest	37.89
				$ 3796.81

The accountants ask allowance for the following disbursements and credits:

Cr.

- By cash paid
    - Philip J. Barnhart for letters: $6.50
    - Z. B. Heindel for proving will: $1.00
    - E. M. Loucks and Martin Sipe, for appraising personal property: $2.00
    - D. W. Cunningham for labor: $1.40
    - The Gazette Co., Ltd., for printing: $4.00
    - G. P. Fisher, for services rendered: $3.00
    - McClellan & Gotwalt, for groceries: $1.67
    - W. H. Miller, auctioneering sale: $10.00
    - Eli Cunningham, for fertilizer: $6.30
    - Z. C. Myers, M.D.: $199.50
    - First National Bank of York, discount on two notes: $3.36
    - Ezra Spangler, collector, county, state and school tax, 1899: $12.68
    - Ezra Spangler, clerking sales of personal property: $2.30
    - Gazette Co., Ltd., for printing and advertising: $5.00
    - Levi Bahn, nursing: $23.50
    - W. H. Miller, auctioneering sale of real estate: $5.00
    - First National Bank of York, note of Albert Cunningham: $80.00
    - Mary Inners, housekeeping: $8.75
    - First National Bank of York, Pa., discount and stamps on note for $147.12: $2.24
    - First National Bank of York, Pa., revenue stamps on sale notes: $0.34

- Fox & Ottmyer, bread and rolls: $2.40
- B. F. Dellinger, flour and feed: $15.88

The accountants ask allowance for the following disbursements and credits:-

Cr.

By cash paid	Philip J. Barnhart for letters	$	6.50
" " "	Z. B. Heindel for proving will		1.00
" " "	R. M. Loucks and Martin Sipe, for appraising personal property		2.00
" " "	D. W. Cunningham for labor		1.40
" " "	The Gazette Co., Ltd., for printing,		4.00
" " "	G. P. Fisher, for services rendered,		3.00
" " "	McClellan & Gotwalt, for groceries,		1.67
" " "	W. H. Miller, auctioneering sale,		10.00
" " "	Eli Cunningham, for fertilizer,		8.30
" " "	Z. C. Myers, M. D.,		19[illegible].50
" " "	First National Bank, of York, discount on two notes,		3.36
" " "	Ezra Spangler, collector, county, State and school tax, 1899,		12.60
" " "	Ezra Spangler, clerking saleof personal property,		2.30
" " "	Gazette Co., Ltd., for printing and advertising,		5.00
" " "	Levi Bahn, nursing,		23.50
" " "	W. H. Miller, auctioneering sale of real estate,		5.00
" " "	First National Bank of York, Pa., note of Albert Cunningham,		80.00
" " "	Mary Inners, house-keeping,		8.75
" " "	First National Bank, York, Pa., discount and stamps on note for $147.12		2.24
" " "	First National Bank, York, Pa., revenue stamps on sale notes,		.34
" " "	Fox & Ottmyer, bread and rolls,		2.40
" " "	B. F. Dellinger, flour and feed		15.8[illegible]

By cash paid	C. J. & W. J. Loucks, screenings,	$ 4.45
" " "	W. H. Miller, auctioneering sale of real estate,	1.00
" " "	First National Bank, York, Pa., note,	147.18
" " "	Franklin Hovis, meat	4.81
" " "	Eli Cunningham, fertilizer and labor,	18.44
" " "	Henry Sleeger & Sons, undertakers,	60.00
" " "	C. Bender & Son, coal bill,	13.50
" " "	Chas. Lichtenberger, tinning,	12.00
" " "	John Sipe,	2.50
" " "	W. D. Miller, auctioneering sale of real estate,	5.00
" " "	H. H. Baughman, lettering monument and foot mark,	8.00
" " "	John LeFevre, county and State tax for 1900,	5.94
" " "	Wm. L. Keech, surveying real estate,	3.00
" " "	Emanuel Spangler, road tax for the year, 1900,	2.50
" " "	Gazette Company, Ltd., printing and advertising,	15.00
" " "	The Security, Title and Trust Co., stamps,	3.50
" " "	John LeFevre, school tax for the year, 1900,	1.97
" " "	Edward and Frank Sipe, digging grave,	2.00
" " "	The Security, Title and Trust Co., school tax for 1901,	.65
" " "	Geo. B. H. Bunt, County and school tax	1.31
" " "	David Cunningham, labor and post,	32.00
" " "	insurance,	7.66
	Edmund Dietz, services rendered to accountants,	15.00
	A. N. Green, professional services,	35.00
	Accountants claim credit for loss on sale of personal property	96.61
" " "	Register for filing appraisement	1.50
	Accountants claim credit for amount due the heirs of Ellen Myers, deceased,	113.00

Final Page Summary:

- **Disbursements and Credits**: Continues to detail various financial transactions and balances related to the estate of William Cunningham.
  - **Verification**: Contains a certification section verifying the accuracy of the accounts, signed by the executors and a register.

By cash paid Register and clerk $ 9.25
Allowance due accountants on the personal estate $28.80
Allowance due accountants on the real estate $84.15
$1129.31
Balance in the hands of the executors $2667.50
$3796.81

York County, ss:
Exhibited into the Register's Office
Affirmed and subscribed to before me this 31st day of October A.D., 1901
Philip J. Barnhart, Register.

Albert Cunningham
David W. Cunningham

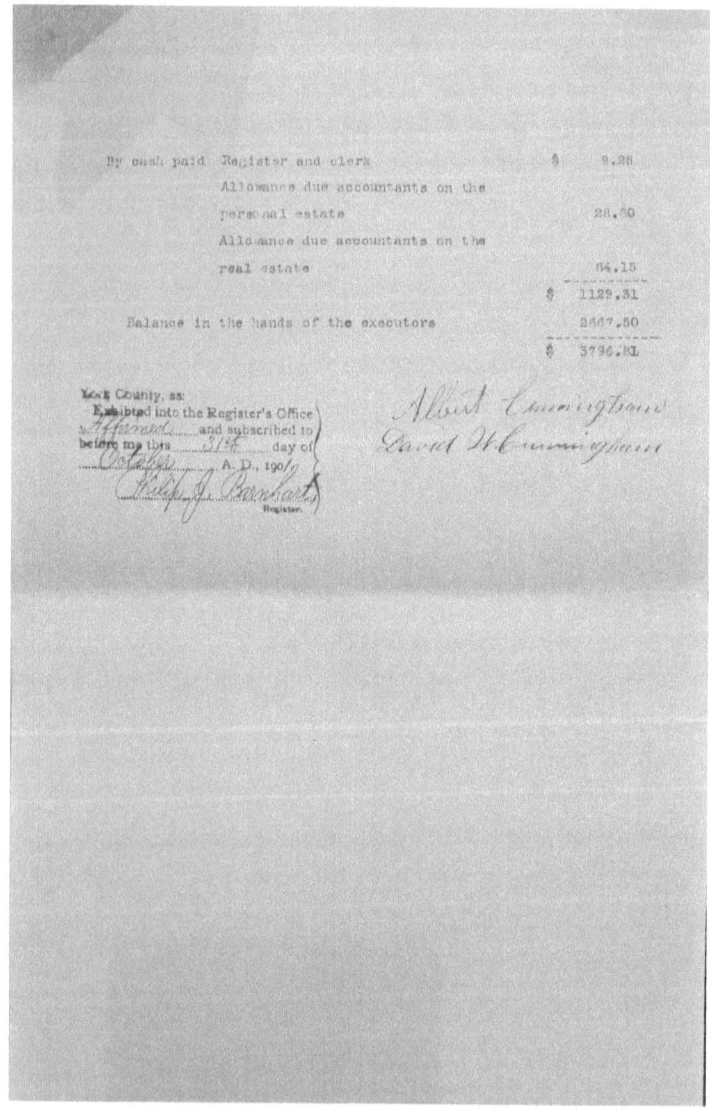

By cash paid	Register and clerk	$	9.28
	Allowance due accountants on the personal estate		28.50
	Allowance due accountants on the real estate		84.15
		$	1129.31
Balance in the hands of the executors			2667.50
		$	3796.81

York County, ss:
Exhibited into the Register's Office
Affirmed and subscribed to
before me this 31st day of
October A. D., 1901
Philip J. Barnhart
Register.

Albert Cunningham
David W. Cunningham

The document from the Orphans' Court of York County is dated December 30, 1901. It pertains to the estate of William

Cunningham, deceased. The court appoints R.E. Cochran, Esq. as the auditor to distribute the balance on the account of Albert Cunningham and D. W. Cunningham, executors of the last will and testament of William Cunningham, late of Spring Garden Township, York County, Pennsylvania. The distribution is to be carried out among those legally entitled to it. The document is signed "By the Court."

In the Orphans' Court of York County.

In the estate of William Cunningham, deceased.

And, now, December 30th, 1901, on motion of A. T. Green, the Court appoint [illegible], Esq., auditor to distribute the balance on the account of Albert Cunningham and D. W. Cunningham, executors of the last will and testament of William Cunningham, late of Spring Garden Township, York County, Penna., deceased, to and among those legally entitled thereto.

By the Court.

3

The Next Generations

The Cunningham Family Legacy

Children of William Cunningham and Lydia Beaverson:

1. Ellen Cunningham
   - (B): Unknown
   - (D): 1892
   - Husband: Horace D. Myers
   - (B): 1853
   - (D): 1884 (age 31)
   - Children:
   - Charles W.
   - Stewart E.: Worked for A.B. Farquhar Works in York, PA
   - Zachariah: Chain maker in York, PA
   - Anna Minerva: Resided with adopted parents, Mr. and Mrs. Henry Kunkle

- Wilber Horace Myers
- (B): December 17, 1881
- (D): Unknown
- Notes: Lived with his uncle George E. Loucks for 20 years, was a violinist in his church choir

2. Albert Cunningham
- (B): July 25, 1856
- (D): December 4, 1931
- First Wife: Ida Agnes Diehl
- (B): August 27, 1858
- (D): May 27, 1904
- Children with Ida Agnes:
- Annie B.
- (B): 1882
- (D): 1886
- Jacob W.: Worked for Pennsylvania Railroad
- (B): 1884
- (D): December 19, 1961
- Married: Alma K. Thompson (Gross) on August 29, 1909 w/son
- Raymond Paul
- (B): July 25, 1898
- (D): Unknown
- Second Wife: Mary Gruver
- (M): January 10, 1909 by Rev. Stump, York, PA
- Child with Mary Gruver:
- Albert
- (B): 1909
- (D): 1909

3. William Cunningham
   - (B): 1858
   - (D): April 9, 1927 in Reading, PA
   - Wife: Almeda Brown
   - (B): December 7, 1856
   - (D): February 22, 1922
   - Son: Harry Brown Cunningham, Sr.
   - (B): July 14, 1879
   - (D): March 17, 1945 in Fayette County, Pennsylvania

4. John P. Cunningham
   - (B): March 30, 1863
   - (D): December 16, 1934
   - Wife: Annie B.
   - (B): October 5, 1865
   - (D): Unknown
   - Children:
   - Horace N.
   - (B): Unknown
   - (D): August 15, 1889
   - Harris N.
   - (B): April 10, 1889
   - (D): August 5, 1889
   - Notes: Possible twins born on the same day, died on different dates
   - Carrie E.
   - (B): August 24, 1885
   - (D): June 28, 1913
   - Elsie B.
   - (B): 1888
   - (D): Unknown

- Notes: Named in the Will and Testament of her grandfather William to inherit money when she turned 21

5. David W. Cunningham
- (B): November 6, 1867
- (D): 1928
- Wife: Ida J.
- (B): 1870
- (D): April 25, 1929 at 5:10 am in York Hospital
- Children:
- Amos G.
- (B): 1895
- (D): June 11, 1911 (16 years, 14 days)
- Florence
- (B): 1890
- (D): 1897
- Lucy
- (B): 1893
- (D): 1899
- Warren H.
- (B): 1897
- (D): Unknown
- Wife: Florence P. Hivey
- (B): Unknown
- (D): November 29, 1946
- (M): December 11, 1920 in York, PA by Rev. Stump when Warren H. was 23 years old
- Robert
- (B): 1907
- (D): 1907
- Jennings (Jim) B.

- (B): Unknown
- (D): Unknown
- Wife: Emma C. Shermeyer
- (B): October 5, 1903
- (D): 1994 (age 91 years)

6. Elizabeth B. Cunningham
   - (B): March 30, 1871
   - (D): December 29, 1880

7. Anna Catherine Cunningham
   - (B): March 30, 1871
   - (D): January 2, 1881
   - Notes: Twins, died 3 days apart

Children of Eli Cunningham and Caroline:

1. Flora Cunningham
   - (D): Died at birth
2. Fannie Cunningham
   - (D): Died at birth
3. Edward
   - (D): Died at birth
4. John E. Cunningham
   - (B): January 9, 1868
   - (D): Unknown
   - Wife: Alice Christ
   - (B): Unknown
   - (D): June 22, 1962 (age 94)
   - (M): September 27, 1891 (at age 23)

5. Emma Cunningham
- (B): July 15, 1869
- (D): Unknown
- (M): Henry Jacob Leckrone in York, PA on April 15, 1888 (at age 18)

6. Walter Cunningham
- (B): February 19, 1875
- (D): 1964
- Wife: Lillie May Snyder
- (B): 1880
- (D): 1954
- Children:
- Helen G.
- (B): March 27, 1900
- (D): December 25, 1900
- Ray
- (B): Unknown
- (D): Unknown

7. Dora Cunningham
- (B): June 22, 1879
- (D): Unknown
- (M): George H. Worley in York, PA on December 25, 1894 (at age 18)
- Children:
- Grace
- (B): Unknown
- (D): Unknown
- Stewart
- (B): Unknown
- (D): Unknown

Walter Cunningham of Springets York Co., Pa.

AND

Lillie M. Snyder of Springets York Co., Pa.

WERE UNITED

IN HOLY MATRIMONY

According to the Ordinance of GOD and the Laws of the State of Pennsylvania at Hellam Pa. on the 29th day of October in the year of OUR LORD One Thousand Eight Hundred and Ninety Nine.

Gideon P. Fisher, Pastor, Hellam, Pa.

Witnesses

Children of David Cunningham and Kate Kohler:

1. Elmira C. Cunningham
 - (B): December 8, 1867 or 1868
 - (D): April 20, 1940
 - (M): Samuel F. Hess on December 1, 1896 (at age 24) by Rev. Kohler
 - (B): March 13, 1873
 - (D): November 22, 195 2. Charles B. Cunningham
 - (B): March 3, 1869
 - (D): June 19, 1958
 - Christened: October 7, 1870
 - First Wife: Emma Stough
 - (B): December 20, 1872
 - (D): February 10, 1916
 - (M): October 19, 1890 in York, PA (at age 21)
 - Children with Emma Stough:
 - Irwin James Cunningham
 - (B): March 6, 1891
 - (D): Unknown
 - Martin Cunningham
 - (B): January 3, 1893
 - (D): 1956
 - (M): Ethel I. Figdore on April 29, 1915 (at age 22)
 - (B): 1894
 - (D): 1950
 - Allen David Cunningham
 - (B): March 31, 1894
 - (D): Unknown
 - Christened: September 23, 1894

 (M) Annie Gross November 20, 1915.

- Katie Irene Cunningham
- (B): March 28, 1898
- (D): 1991
- (M): Clarence E. Raffensberger on January 27, 1917 (at age 20)
- Notes: Their son Ken played in Major League Baseball for the Chicago Cubs
- Louise Rebecca Cunningham
- (B): June 2, 1900
- (D): Unknown
- Christened: August 22, 1900
- Second Wife: Minnie Rauhouser
- (M): January 5, 1918 in York, PA by Rev. Stump (at age 48)

3. William A. Cunningham
   - (B): Unknown
   - (D): December 25, 1870
   - Wife: Iva C. Spangler
   - (B): Unknown
   - (D): January 2, 1926
   - (M): May 1, 1910 (at age 23)
   - Daughter: Mary Ann Cunningham
   - (B): 1924
   - (D): 1924

4. James Franklin Cunningham
   - (B): February 22, 1871
   - (D): 1951
   - Wife: Elizabeth F.
   - (B): 1875
   - (D): 1935

- Children:
- Nettie Irene Cunningham
- (B): August 4, 1895
- (D): Unknown
- (M): Charles C. Mohr on November 13, 1915 in York, PA by Rev. Enders (at age 20)
- Anna May Cunningham
- (B): January 8, 1899
- (D): Unknown
- (M): Paul Joseph Gross on June 16, 1917 (at age 18)
- Ruth E. Cunningham
- (B): 1905
- (D): January 27, 1990

5. Nettie M. Cunningham
   - (B): Unknown
   - (D): Unknown
   - (M): G. Henry Moul on February 11, 1902 in York, PA by Rev. Stump (at age 23)

6. Susan Rebecca Cunningham
   - (B): January 17, 1877
   - (D): Unknown
   - Christened: April 11, 1879
   - (M): Edgar Hykes on April 7, 1901 in York, PA by Rev. Stump (at age 23)

7. David Luther Cunningham
   - (B): October 17, 1879
   - (D): Unknown
   - Christened: October 16, 1880

- (M): Emma Boyer on December 25, 1905 in York, PA by Rev. Stump

8. George Cunningham
   - (B): Unknown
   - (D): Unknown

4

Modern Era: The Cunningham Descendants

William and Almeda (Brown) Cunningham Lineage

Family of Almeda (Brown) Cunningham

Father: Charles Murray

(B) June 10, 1816

(D) April 30, 1898

Notes: Deacon of St. John Lutheran Church in Maytown, PA. Made chairs and spinning wheels.

(M) Sara Ann

(B) April 25, 1824

(D) November 4, 1894

Children: All baptized at St. John Lutheran Church

Son: William H.

(B) 1854 (D) unknown

Daughter: Emma Almeda

(B) December 7, 1856

(D) February 22, 1922 or 23 in Dawson, PA. Her son, Harry Brown Cunningham, Sr. , took her body by train to be buried at St. John Lutheran Church, Maytown, PA. (Lancaster County).

Daughter: Leah Rebecca

(B) 1859 (D) unknown (M) Peter Raum

Daughter: Frances Viola

(B) 1863 (D) unknown (M) Mr. Salteman

Daughter: Mary

(B) unknown (D) unknown (M) George Edward Ohler

Notes: Charles M. Brown possibly had a brother:

John F. Brown (B) 1846 (D) 1925

Wife: Charlotte (B) 1836 (D) 1925

Children:

Lottie Almeda

Clara May

Children and Grandchildren of William and Almeda (Brown) Cunningham

Harry Brown Cunningham, Sr.**

- (B): July 14, 1879

- (D): March 17, 1945 in Fayette County, PA in a mental institution, following the death of his son William in Italy during WW2.

- Christened: February 13, 1881 by Rev. A. Wanner, possibly in St. John Lutheran Church in Maytown, PA

- Parents: William Cunningham (B: 1858, D: April 9, 1927 in Reading, PA) and Emma Almeda Brown (B: December 7, 1856, D: February 22, 1922 or 1923 in Dawson, PA)

First Marriage: Sadie E. Druck

- (B): 1883

- (D): September 28, 1913 in York, PA

- Married: October 12, 1901 by Rev. H.C. Salem, residence in Brogue (Chanceford Township), PA in York County.

- Father: William Aaron Druck

(B) 1855 (D) 1883

- Mother: Priscilla J.

(B) 1859 (D) 1892

- Child:

- Elsie M.

- (B) May 19, 1902 Brogue (Chanceford Township) York, PA

- (D): 1997 (age 95)

- Notes: Supposedly raised by an aunt after Sadie (Mother) died.

- (M): Elmer Hess

- (B): 1907

- (D): 1994 (age 87)

Notes: Elmer worked as a mason for William Druck who owned a Mason business. Elsie was working in a cigar factory as a cigar roller. Elsie's grandmother Almeda (Brown) Cunningham was a machine operator in the cigar factory. Supposedly, Elmer was a avid cigar smoker. 1940 census shows Elmer Hess occupation: Mason, earning $800/year. Elsie Hess occupation: cigar roller, earning $405/year.

Children of Elmer and Elsie:

- Evelyn Donna (Sheffer) (B) 1932 (D) 2014
- Nancy L. (Eaton) (B) 1926 (D) 2014

Second Marriage: Mary McGinnis

- (B): 1896

- (D): November 17, 1973 in Fayette County, PA

Children:

1. - Geraldine

- (B): 1919

- (D): 1994 age 75

- (M): Wayne Howard

2. - Harry Brown Cunningham, Jr.

- (B): December 17, 1920

- (D): September 29, 1985

Notes: An avid fiddle player who participated in fiddle competitions in the Tri-State area of Pennsylvania, West Virginia, and Ohio.

-(M) Eva Mae Shallenberger

(B) June 17, 1916 (D) April 22, 1955

- -Children:
- -Anna Mary
- -Doris Louise
- -Nelda Mae
- -Charles
- -Roy Brown

3. - George William Cunningham

- (B): March 9, 1922

- (D): July 17, 1944 (died in Italy during WW2)

4. - Reba

- (B): June 21, 1926

- (D): August 15, 1994

5. - Joyce

- (B): January 31, 1930
- (D): November 30, 1996

Harry Brown Cunningham Sr.

The sepia-toned photograph captures Harry Brown Cunningham Sr. standing next to a large cannon in what appears to be a park or open area. Dressed in a suit and hat, with one arm resting on the cannon, Harry Brown Cunningham Sr. embodies a distinguished and historical presence.

Family Gathering Photo

The photo captures a family gathering, arranged in front of a barn and silo. The image includes two rows of individuals with the following names:

First Row (Left to Right):

1. Nancy Hess
2. Evelyn Hess
3. Eva Mae Cunningham
4. Joyce Cunningham
5. Aunt Elsie Hess

Second Row (Left to Right):

1. Wayne Howard
2. Reba Cunningham
3. Geraldine Howard
4. Elmer Hess (Uncle)
5. H.B. Cunningham Jr.
6. Bill Cunningham (George William)
7. H.B. Cunningham Sr.

Family Photo: Mary (McGinnis) Cunningham and Descendants

The black-and-white photograph captures three generations of the Cunningham family. Seated on the left is Mary (McGinnis) Cunningham. Beside Mary almost sitting on her lap is grandson Roy Brown Cunningham and next is his brother Charles Cunningham with their father Harry Brown Cunningham Jr. (Mary's son)

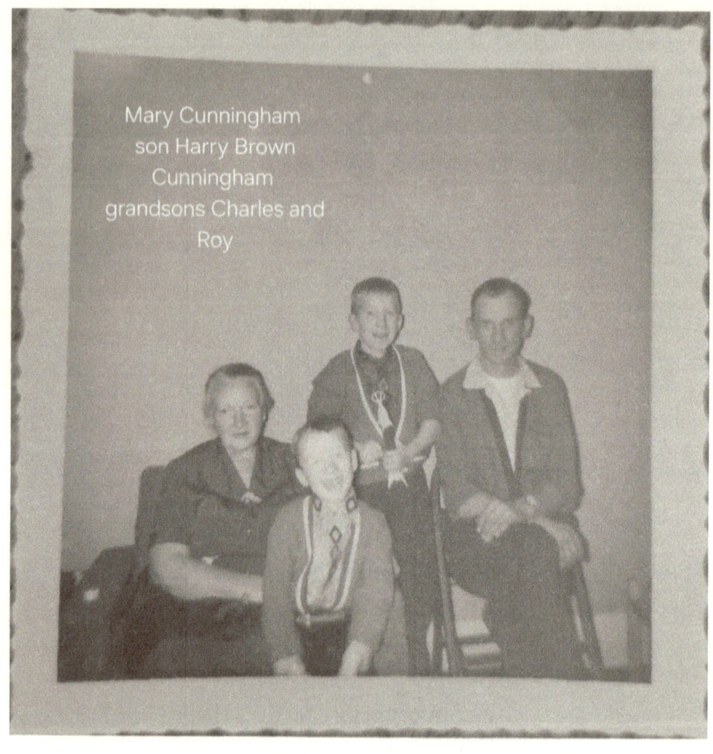
Mary Cunningham
son Harry Brown
Cunningham
grandsons Charles and
Roy

5

Genealogy Resources

To authenticate the family genealogy, a variety of resources were consulted. Libraries and historical societies provided invaluable access to newspaper clippings on microfilm, historical books, and census records. This chapter highlights some of the specific information used to confirm family lineage, including birth dates, death dates, marriage dates, and the names and ages of children recorded in census documents.

Note: In some cases, census records contained errors, such as misspelled names or incorrect ages, which hindered the process of corroborating information. While most corrections were made using available resources, some data remains elusive.

Below is a 1850 census of the John Spangler household. It shows the son of John and Elizabeth Cunningham, William, living there as a laborer in his grandfather's home.

The 1880 census will show William living with own family and their children along with this one brother Eli living with his own family.

1850 CENSUS

Spangler, John 73 farmer Pa./Springgarden Twp. 170/220/239
Christiann 65
Eliza Frey 16 in household
*Wm. Cunningham 18 Pa. laborer
Wm. Frey 17 Pa laborer
Sarah Spangler 10 Pa.

1880 CENSUS - Spring Garden Twp. 3-18-1918
Cunningham

Eli	wm	42	Farmer	m Pa
Caroline	wf	40	wife	m Pa
John E.	wm	12	son	
Emma	wf	10	dau.	
Walter	wm	5	son	
Dora	wf	11 mos.	dau.	

1880 CENSUS
Cunningham

William	wm	47		m	Pa
Lydia	wf	48		m	Pa.
John	wm	17	son	s	Pa
David	wm	13	son	s	Pa
Elizabeth	wf	[illegible]	dau.	s	Pa
Anna C.	wf	9	dau.	s	Pa

PAGE 1

The next images will be of a series of family index cards found at the Mt. Zion Lutheran Cemetery. These confirmed other family connections.

Cunningham, George
died F 5 1867. 32-6-7.
" , Georgieann
dau. of Georgie & Maggie
died F 14 1867. 28 days.
" , Laura V., dau. of George & Maggie
died O 10 1866. 1-11-0.
" , Rebecca E.,
died Mr 25 1863. 5 days.

Mt. Zion Springettsbury Twp.

CUNNINGHAM
Cunningham, David S. 1867 - 1928
" , Ida J., his wife, 1870 - 1929
" , Amos (son) 1895 - 1911
" , Florence (daughter) 1890 - 1897
" , Lucy (") 1893 - 1899
" , Robert (son) 1907 - 1907
" , Infants 1905 - 1909

Mt. Zion Springettsbury Twp.

CUNNINGHAM
Cunningham, -----, son of Warren & Florence
died J 11 1926 (only date given)
" , Paul W.
died Je 24 1921 (only date given)
(both wooden markers)

Mt. Zion Springettsbury Twp.

CUNNINGHAM
Cunningham, Eli
Je 10 1837 - N 26 1913
" , Caroline, his wife
Ap 3 1840 - Ja 8 1913
" , George (no dates given)
(TWINS)

Mt. Zion Springettsbury Twp.

CUNNINGHAM
Cunningham, John F.
Mr 30 1863 - N 16 1934
" , Annie, his wife
born O 5 1865 (only date given)
" , Horrace N., their son
died Ag 15 1889; 0-4-5
" , Harris N., Ap 10 1889-Ag 5 1889
" , Carrie E., Ag 24 1885-Je 28 1913

Mt. Zion Springettsbury Twp.

CUNNINGHAM
Cunningham, Emma
D 20 1872 - F 10 1916
" , Iva C., died Ja 2 1926; 53-7-1
" , Mary A.,
died Mr 31 1924 (only date given)
" , Elizabeth Frances
died F 20 1930; 59-9-28
" , Urie M., died Ag 3 1909; 2-3-9.
" , Helen M., dau. of Walter & Lillie
Mr 27 1900 - D 28 1900; 0-9-1.

Mt. Zion Springettsbury Twp.

CUNNINGHAM
Cunningham, John E.
born 1868 (only date given)
" , Alice, his wife
born 1867 (only date given)
" , Bruce R., their son
1894 - 1923
(Co.A.304th Eng'rs. 79th Div.)

Mt. Zion Springettsbury Twp.

CUNNINGHAM
Cunningham, Flora)
" , Fannie) children of Eli & Caroline
" , Edward)
" , John; died Je 29 1866. 66-6-3
" , Elizabeth Spangler (wife)
O 17 1812 - Mr 7 1883. 70-4-20.
Dau. of John & (Hastine Schultz) Spangler

Mt. Zion Springettsbury Twp.

CUNNINGHAM

Cunningham, William (wooden marker)
died Ap 9 1927; 69-0-26

" , David; died D 3 1908; 69-1-21.

" , Kate C., wife of David
died N 27 1919; 76-1-10

" , Henry A., son of David & Kate C.
died O 25 1873; 0-9-4.

" , Albert; Jl 25 1856 - D 4 1931

" , Ida Agnes
Ag 27 1858 - My 27 1904

" , Annie B., 1882 - 1886

" , Albert; 1909 - 1909

Mt. Zion Springettsbury Twp.

CUNNINGHAM

Cunningham, Wm. 4:30pm
died Jl 25 1899; 66-11-21 born (4 Aug 1832)

" , Lydia A., his wife born
died D 10 1894; 62-6-29 (12 May 1832)

" , Elizabeth A.
died D 29 1880; 9-11-24

" , Catharine A.
died Ja 2 1881; 9-11-27

" , 2 twin daus. of Wm. & Lydia A.
(no dates given)

Mt. Zion Springettsbury Twp.

The next image will be a listing of obituaries. Only two have direct connection to this Cunningham lineage that can be corroborated (marked with asterisks). That of a George E Cunningham, son of David and Katie Cunningham.

The other of William Cunningham, the son of William and Lydia Cunningham, who died in Reading, PA and eventually buried in Mt. Zion Lutheran Cemetery.

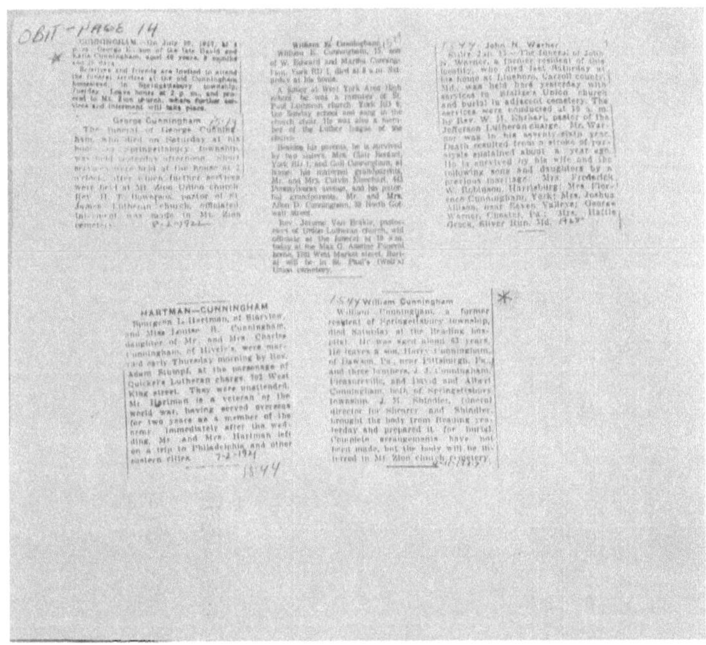

OBIT - PAGE 14

CUNNINGHAM — On July [illegible], 19[illegible], at [illegible] p. m., George E., son of the late David and [illegible] Cunningham, aged [illegible] years, [illegible] months and [illegible] days.

Relatives and friends are invited to attend the funeral services at the old Cunningham homestead, in Springettsbury township, Tuesday. Leave house at 2 p. m., and proceed to Mt. Zion church, where further services and interment will take place.

George Cunningham

The funeral of George Cunningham, who died on Saturday at his home in Springettsbury township, was held yesterday afternoon. Short services were held at the house at 2 o'clock, after which further services were held at Mt. Zion Union church. Rev. H. T. [illegible], pastor of St. James Lutheran church, officiated. Interment was made in Mt. Zion cemetery.

William E. Cunningham

William E. Cunningham, 15, son of W. Edward and Martha Cunningham, York RD 1, died at 8 a.m. Saturday at his home.

A [illegible] at West York Area High school, he was a member of St. Paul Lutheran church, York RD [illegible], the Sunday school and sang in the church choir. He was also a member of the Luther league of the church.

Besides his parents, he is survived by two sisters, Mrs. [illegible], York RD 1, and [illegible] Cunningham, at home; his maternal grandparents, Mr. and Mrs. Calvin [illegible], [illegible] Pennsylvania avenue, and his paternal grandparents, Mr. and Mrs. Allen D. Cunningham, [illegible] North [illegible] street.

Rev. Jerome Van Brakle, pastor of Union Lutheran church, will officiate at the funeral at 10 a.m. today at the Max G. [illegible] Funeral home, [illegible] West Market street. Burial will be in St. Paul's (Wolf's) Union cemetery.

John N. Warner

[illegible], Jan. 13.—The funeral of John N. Warner, a former resident of this locality, who died last Saturday at his home at [illegible], Carroll county, Md., was held here yesterday with services in [illegible] Union church and burial in adjacent cemetery. The services were conducted at 10 a. m. by Rev. W. H. [illegible], pastor of the Jefferson Lutheran charge. Mr. Warner was in his seventy-sixth year. Death resulted from a stroke of paralysis sustained about a year ago. He is survived by his wife and the following sons and daughters by a previous marriage: Mrs. Frederick W. Robinson, Harrisburg; Mrs. Florence Cunningham, York; Mrs. Joshua Allison, near Seven Valleys; George Warner, Chester, Pa.; Mrs. Hattie Druck, Silver Run, Md.

HARTMAN—CUNNINGHAM

[illegible] L. Hartman, of [illegible], and Miss Louise H. Cunningham, daughter of Mr. and Mrs. Charles Cunningham, of [illegible], were married early Thursday morning by Rev. Adam Stump, at the parsonage of Quickel's Lutheran charge, [illegible] West King street. They were unattended. Mr. Hartman is a veteran of the world war, having served overseas for two years as a member of the army. Immediately after the wedding, Mr. and Mrs. Hartman left on a trip to Philadelphia and other eastern cities.

William Cunningham

William Cunningham, a former resident of Springettsbury township, died Saturday at the Reading hospital. He was aged about [illegible] years. He leaves a son, Harry Cunningham, of Dawson, Pa., near Pittsburgh, Pa., and three brothers, J. J. Cunningham, [illegible], and David and Albert Cunningham, both of Springettsbury township. J. M. Shindler, funeral director for Shearer and Shindler, brought the body from Reading yesterday and prepared it for burial. Complete arrangements have not been made, but the body will be interred in Mt. Zion church cemetery.

Another set of family index cards pertaining to Harry Brown Cunningham, Sr. There is still some uncertainty with the mother of Sadie E. Druck. One online source has her name as Priscilla J., but this one card file has a Amanda listed.

Control CUNNINGHAM　　Source 372 Book T Page 407
Name CUNNINGHAM, HARRY B.
Residence BROGUEVILLE, YORK CO., PA – CHANCEFORD TWP
Born Age 22 yr　at
Baptized　Sponsors
Church membership(s)
612　offices
Married 14 OCT 1901　at THE PARSONAGE　Rocky
by Rev. H.C. SALEM　witnesses
Died　aged　at
Buried
Father WILLIAM
Mother
Spouse SADIE E. DUCK
Children
ELSIE M.　B. MAY 19, 1902　Brogue, CHANCEFORD TWP, YORK, PA
D.　1997, YORK, PA Age 95
M. ELMER HESS
Children: NANCY L. 1936–2014　EVELYN DONNA (SHAFFER) 1932–2014

Age marriage

CALENDAR OF VITAL RECORDS OF THE COUNTIES OF YORK AND ADAMS
THE HISTORICAL SOCIETY OF YORK COUNTY

CONTROL: CUNNINGHAM

NAME CUNNINGHAM, Harry B.
RESIDENCE
DATE OF BIRTH July 13,1879　PLACE
DATE OF CHRISTENING Feb.13,1881　PLACE by Rev. A. Wanner
DATE OF MARRIAGE　PLACE
DATE OF DEATH　PLACE
DATE OF BURIAL　PLACE
FATHER William
MOTHER E.A.
SPONSORS
SPOUSES

Mount Zion, Springettsbury Twp., York Co., Pa.

ADDITIONAL INFORMATION MAY BE GIVEN ON THE BACK.

Control CUNNINGHAM　　Source YORK COUNTY COURT HOUSE MARRIAGE LICENSE DOCKET Book T Page 407
Name CUNNINGHAM, Harry B. Born 1879
Residence Chanceford Twp.
Born Age 22yr　at
Baptized　Sponsors
Church membership(s)
offices
Married 12 Oct. 1901　at Rockey
by Rev. Salem　witnesses
Died　aged　at
Buried
Father William
Mother Amanda
Spouse Sadie E. Druck
Children

A 1900 census shows a Sadie E. Druck, age 16, born in 1883 living with a William Druck, believed to be father, no mention of mother. However, the one online source that mentions her mother being: Priscilla J. was born in 1859 and died in 1892, which would confirm in the 1900 census, the mother would have already died when census taken.

Let's forward to the 1940 census. It shows:

William Druck age 50, born in 1890.
Wife: Minnie age 45
Daughter: Margaret age 23
Son: Charles age 22
Note: This William Druck is believed to be a brother to Sadie E. Druck. William Druck was the owner of a Masonry business. His son Charles was the co-owner.

William Druck owned his home, living at 142 S. Franklin Street, Red Lion, PA.

Elmer Hess was living at 140 S. Franklin Street, Red Lion, PA. Other side of double house, renting from William Druck. 1940 census shows:

Elmer Hess age 33
Wife: Elsie age 36? Possible typo of 38.
Daughter: Evelyn Donna age 8
Daughter: Nancy L. Age 3
Note: Elmer worked as a mason for William Druck. Elsie was working in a cigar factory as a cigar roller. Elsie's grandmother Almeda Brown Cunningham was a machine operator in the cigar factory. 1940 census shows Elmer Hess occupation as Mason, earning $800/year and Elsie Hess occupation as cigar roller, earning $405/year.

The 1940 census also shows a Roy Hess working in a cigar factory, earning $800/year along with Violet Hess working in the cigar factory, earning $190/year. Living at 116 S. Franklin

Street, Red Lion, PA along with a Mirian living in the household.

Burial Records and Cemetery Listings

The burial records at Mt. Zion Lutheran Church Cemetery provide further insight into the Cunningham family. Notable entries include:

- William Cunningham (wooden marker) died on April 9, 1927.
- David Cunningham died on December 3, 1908.
- Kate C., wife of David, died November 27, 1919.
- Albert Cunningham, born July 25, 1856 – died December 4, 1931.
- Ida Agnes Cunningham, born August 27, 1855 – died May 27, 1904.
- Annie D. Cunningham, 1882–1886.
- Albert Cunningham Jr., 1909–1909.

Further confirmation and details on the family's history are supported by census data, probate records, and burial listings.

The following will be photos of some of the Cunningham grave markers found at the Mt. Zion Lutheran Cemetery in Springettsbury Township, PA.

John Cunningham and Mt. Zion Lutheran Church

John Cunningham, originally from Maryland, played a significant role in the establishment of Mt. Zion Lutheran Church in

Springettsbury Township, York County, PA. After settling in the area, he not only cleared and cultivated his 104-acre property but also contributed to the construction of the church. His efforts helped lay the foundation for the community's spiritual and social life.

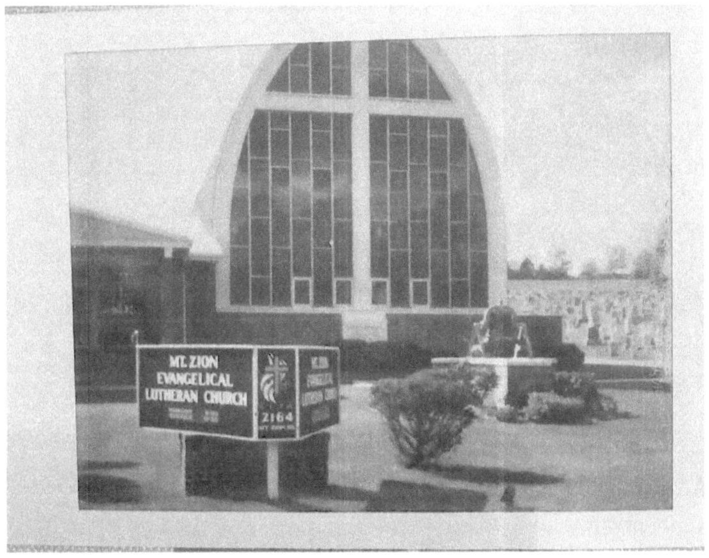

Mt. Zion Lutheran Church

Cornerstone

- Original Cornerstone Inscription: 1851
    - Rebuilt: 1880

The cornerstone signifies the historical importance of Mt. Zion

Lutheran Church, which John Cunningham helped establish. The church was originally built in 1851 and later rebuilt in 1880, serving as a vital part of the community in Springettsbury Township, York County, PA.

Grave Marker of John and Elizabeth (Spangler) Cunningham

The grave marker shows the resting place of John Cunningham and his wife Elizabeth (Spangler) Cunningham. The inscription, though weathered, provides a tangible connection to their lives and legacy in Springettsbury Township, York County, PA.

John Spangler

John Spangler was the father of Elizabeth (Spangler) Cunningham. He played a significant role in the early history of the Spangler family in Pennsylvania. His contributions to the family and community are remembered and honored by his descendants.

John. SPANGLER

John and Christina Spangler

John Spangler and his wife Christina (Christine) Spangler were the parents of Elizabeth (Spangler) Cunningham, who married John Cunningham. Their legacy is preserved through their daughter Elizabeth and her descendants. The grave marker of Christina Spangler provides a tangible connection to the family's history.

CHRISTINA SPANGLER

Grave Marker of William Cunningham and Lydia Cunningham

William Cunningham
- Role: Ex-County Commissioner

Lydia Cunningham
- Wife of William Cunningham

The grave markers beside them also mentions:
- Elizabeth A. and Catherine A., twin daughters of William and Lydia Cunningham

The inscription highlights William Cunningham's role as a county commissioner and commemorates the family's legacy in the region.

William + Lydia
X County Comm

ELIZABETH A } twin
CATHERINE A } daus
of Wm + Lydia

Grave Marker of Eli and Caroline Cunningham

Eli Cunningham
- (B): June 10, 1837
- (D): November 25, 1913
- Notes: Eli was the son of William Cunningham, Ex-County Commissioner.

Caroline Cunningham (Wife)
- (B): April 3, 1840
- (D): June 8, 1913

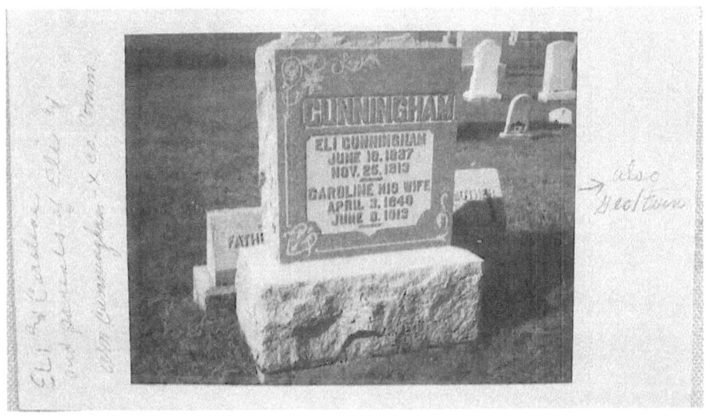

Grave Marker of the Children of Eli and Caroline Cunningham

This grave marker honors the children of Eli and Caroline Cunningham, who are buried beside their grandparents, John and Christina Spangler.

Grave Marker of Walter and Lillie M. Cunningham

Walter Cunningham
- (B): 1875
- (D): 1964

Note: Son of Eli and Caroline Cunningham

Lillie M. Cunningham (Wife)
- (B): 1880
- (D): 1954

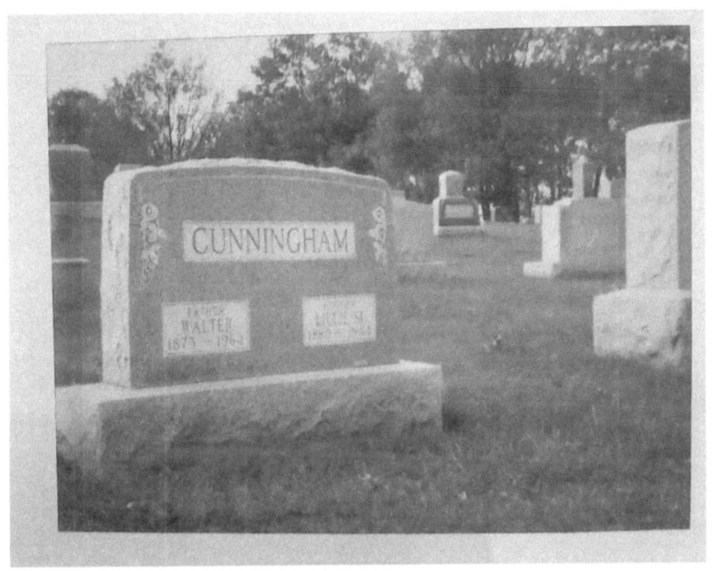

Grave Marker of John E., Alice, and Bruce R. Cunningham

John E. Cunningham
- (B): 1868
- (D): 1934

Note: Son of Eli and Caroline Cunningham

Alice Cunningham (Wife)
- (B): 1867

- (D): 1962

Bruce R. Cunningham (Son)

- (B): 1894
- (D): 1923
- Military Service: CO. A 304TH ENGRS. 79TH DIV.

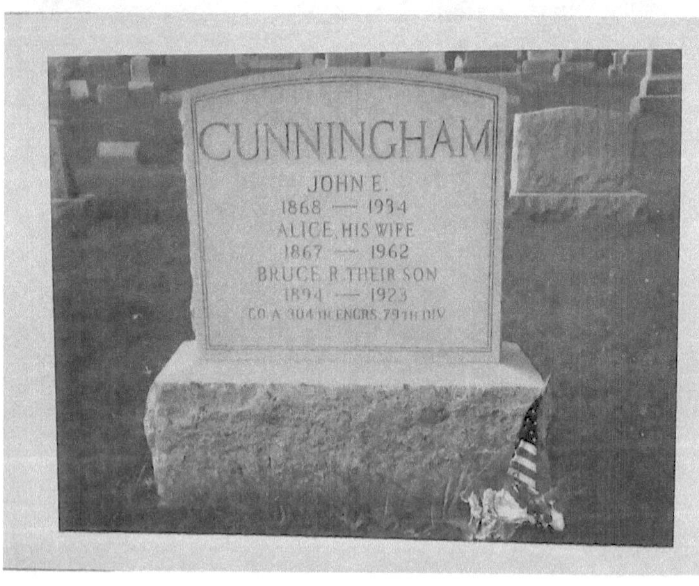

Grave Marker of Albert Cunningham and His Wife Ida Agnes

Albert Cunningham
- (B): July 23, 1856
- (D): December 4, 1931
- Note: Albert was the son of William Cunningham, who served as a County Commissioner.

Ida Agnes Cunningham
- (B): August 27, 1858
- (D): May 27, 1904
- Note: Wife of Albert Cunningham

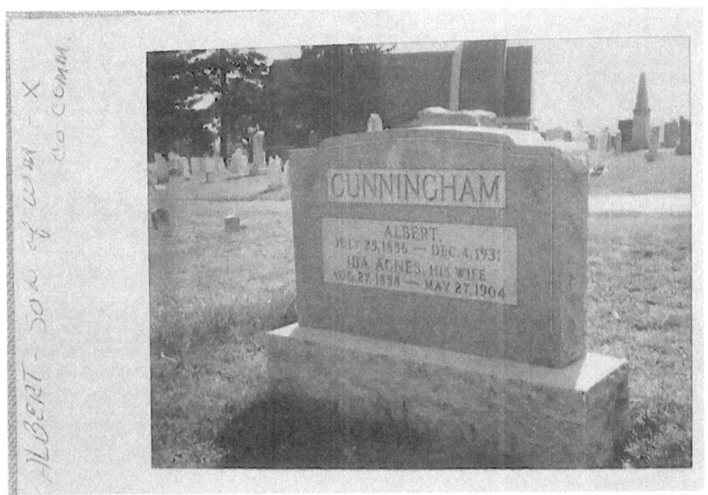

Grave Marker of David and Kate Cunningham

David Cunningham
- (B): October 12, 1839
- (D): December 3, 1908
- Notes: Brother of William Cunningham, Ex-County Commissioner

Kate (Kohler) (Wife)
- (B): 1843
- (D): November 27, 1919 age 75

Grave Marker of Charles and Emma Cunningham

Charles B. Cunningham
- (B): March 3, 1869
- (D): June 15, 1958

Note: Son of David and Kate (Kohler) Cunningham

Emma (Stough) Cunningham
- (B): December 20, 1872
- (D): February 10, 1915

Grave Marker of James F., Elizabeth F., and Ruth E. Cunningham

James F. Cunningham

- (B): 1871
- (D): 1951

Note: Son of David and Kate (Kohler) Cunningham

Elizabeth F. Cunningham (Wife)

- (B): 1878
- (D): 1935

Ruth E. Cunningham (Daughter)

- (B): 1905
- (D): 1990

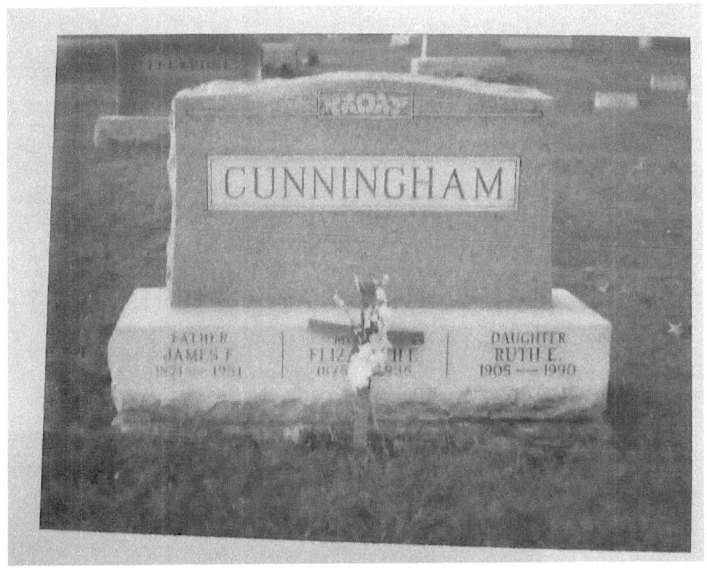

Grave Marker of Katie Irene Cunningham Raffensberger and Clarence E. Raffensberger

Katie Irene (Cunningham) Raffensberger
- (B): 1898
- (D): 1991
- Notes: Daughter of Charles B. Cunningham, married to Clarence E. Raffensberger. They had a son, Ken Raffensberger, who played Major League Baseball for the Chicago Cubs.

Clarence E. Raffensberger
- (B): 1897
- (D): 1982

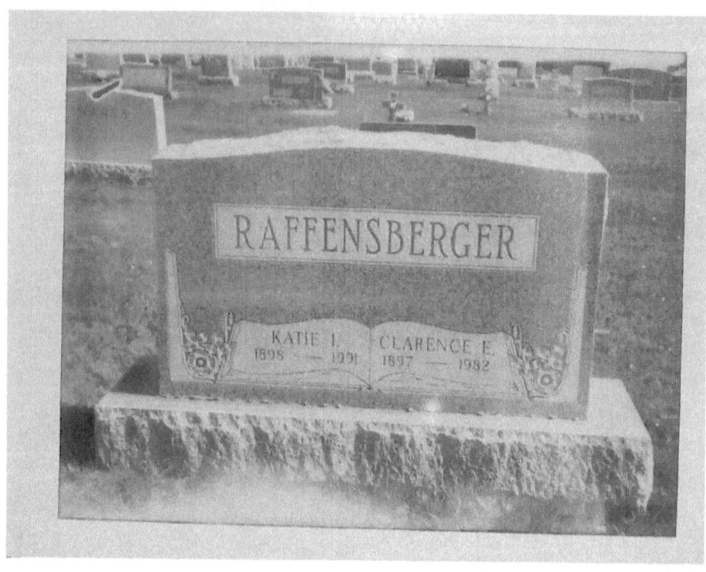

Grave Marker of Martin and Ethel Cunningham

Martin Cunningham
- (B): 1893
- (D): 1956

NOTE: Grandson of David and Kate Cunningham

Ethel I. Cunningham (wife)
- (B): 1894 (D): 1950

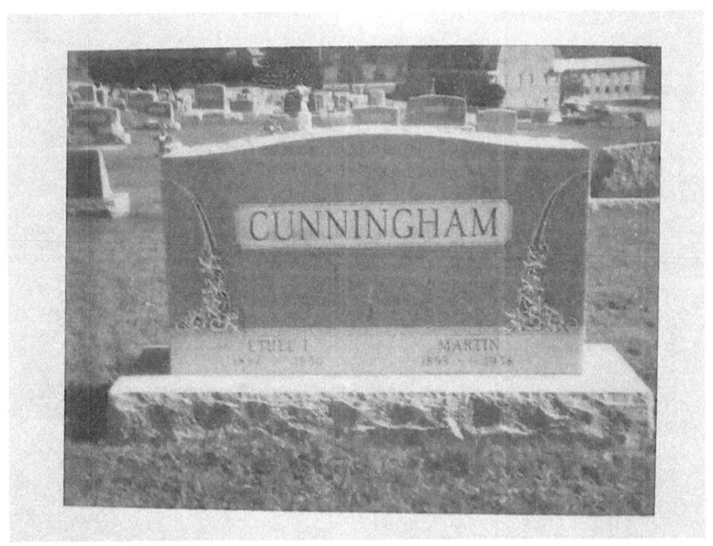

Grave Marker of David W. and Ida J. Cunningham and Their Children

David W. Cunningham
- (B): 1867
- (D): 1928

Note: Son of William Cunningham Ex-County Commissioner

Ida J. Cunningham (Wife)
- (B): 1870
- (D): 1929

Their Children:
- Amos: 1895 - 1911

- Florence: 1890 - 1897
- Lucy: 1893 - 1899
- Robert: 1902 - 1907
- Infants: 1905 - 1909

Cunningham Family Newspaper Announcements

1544 William Cunningham

William Cunningham, a former resident of Springettsbury township, died Saturday at the Reading hospital. He was aged about 63 years. He leaves a son, Harry Cunningham, of Dawson, Pa., near Pittsburgh, Pa., and three brothers, J. J. Cunningham, Pleasureville, and David and Albert Cunningham, both of Springettsbury township. J. M. Shindler, funeral director for Shearer and Shindler, brought the body from Reading yesterday and prepared it for burial. Complete arrangements have not been made, but the body will be interred in Mt. Zion church cemetery.

4-11-1927

MRS. ALBERT CUNNINGHAM.

1-20-1917 1544

Mrs. Mary Cunningham, fifty-three years old, wife of Albert Cunningham, died at the home of her brother-in-law, Adam Ness, 619 West King street, yesterday morning at 11:45 o'clock, after a sickness which began the early part of last September, and was due to a complication of diseases. She is survived by her husband, one son, Elmer Gruver, of Philadelphia; three sisters, Mrs. Adam Ness, of York; Mrs. Martha Krout, of York Haven, and Mrs. Sarah Rehman, of Spring Grove; and two brothers, Daniel Sheffer, of Baltimore, and Henry Sheffer, near Dover. The funeral services will be held at the house at 1:30 o'clock tomorrow afternoon, after which the funeral party will proceed to Wolfe's church, where private interment will be made. Rev. Dr. W. H. Feldmann, pastor of Union Lutheran church will officiate. The funeral will be in charge of Undertaker Dotterer.

MRS. IDA CUNNINGHAM, OF PLEASUREVILLE, DIES

1929

Pleasureville, April 25.—Mrs. Ida J. Cunningham, widow of David W. Cunningham, died this morning at 5:10 o'clock at the York hospital where she had been a patient for some time. She was 59 years old. She leaves the following children: Jennings B. Cunningham, Warren H. Cunningham, Mrs. Jacob Billet and Mrs. Maurice Holler, all of York, R. D. No. 5. Also these brothers and sisters. William Inerst, New York; Harvey Inerst, John Inerst and C. C. Inerst, all of York, R. D. No. 5; Mrs. Delph Wolfgang and Mrs. Samuel Rauhauser, North York. Eight grandchildren also survive.

Funeral services will be conducted at the home of her son-in-law and daughter, Mr. and Mrs. Maurice Holler, Pleasureville, at 2 o'clock Sunday afternoon. Concluding services will be conducted in the Pleasureville United Brethren church. Rev. D. R. Fair will officiate. Interment will take place in Mt. Zion cemetery. Shearer and Shindler, North York funeral directors ,removed the body from the hospital.

Mrs. William A. Cunningham 15544

Mrs. Ida Spangler Cunningham, wife of William A. Cunningham, died Saturday night at 9:30 o'clock at her late residence at York R. D. 5, Springettsbury avenue. Death followed a several days' illness of a complication of diseases. She was aged 36 years, 7 months and 1 day.

She leaves, besides her husband, her father, Jacob Spangler, of Mt. Zion and the following brothers and sisters: Walter Spangler, Mt. Zion; Milton Spangler, of the Glades; Charles Spangler, Windsor Park; Mrs. William Shriver, Emigsville; Mrs. Jacob Yinger, North York and Mrs. Oliver Garbrick, of Springetts.

The funeral will be held on Wednesday afternoon, leaving the house at 1 o'clock. Proceed to Mt. Zion church, where services will be held. Interment will take place in the cemetery adjoining the church.

1-4-1926

tery. Dis — 6/22/62

Mrs. Alice C. Cunningham

Mrs. Alice Crist Cunningham, widow of John E. Cunningham, died at her residence, 2099 North Sherman street, at 5:13 p. m. yesterday at the age of 94. 1544

Mrs. Cunningham was the oldest member of the congregation of Mt. Zion United Church of Christ.

She is survived by four children, Mrs. Molly Linebaugh and Caroline P. Cunningham, 2099 North Sherman; Eli C. Cunningham, York R. D. 7; and Chester E. Cunningham, 1933 Susquehanna Trail north; two grandchildren, Mrs. James Livingston, York R. D. 7, and Mrs. Howard Atkins, Newmanstown; nine great-grandchildren, and a sister, Mrs. Annie Unger, 1885 Andrews street.

Mrs. Cunningham's pastor, the Rev. William Anderson, will officiate at the funeral services at 2 p. m. Sunday at Mt. Zion church. Interment will be in Mt. Zion Cemetery.

The Sleeger Funeral Home, 822 East Market street, is in charge of arrangements.

Raymond P. Cunningham

HALLAM — Raymond P. Cunningham, 82, of 276 E. Market St., formerly of Wrightsville, died Saturday at Memorial Osteopathic Hospital.

He was the husband of the late EMma Rider Cunningham.

Mr. Cunningham, born in Pleasureville, was the son of the late Albert and Ida Diehl Cunningham.

He was a retired employee of Beacon Milling Co., York, and had been employed previously by the New York Wire Cloth Co. He was a member of Trinity United Church of Christ.

Survivors include:

A daughter — Verna L. Witman, 276 E. Market St.

A son — Clifford J. Cunningham, 16 E. Maple St., East Prospect.

Twelve grandchildren and 11 great-grandchildren.

Funeral services will be at 2 p.m. Tuesday at Etzweiler Funeral Home, 1111 E. Market St., with the Rev. Dean Feather, pastor of Trinity UCC, officiating. Burial will be in Mt. Zion Cemetery.

Memorial contributions may be made to Trinity United Church of Christ, 200 E. Market St., Hallam 17406.

York Dispatch Monday July 13 1981

15th

12/26/61 Y.D. 1544

Jacob W. Cunningham

Jacob W. Cunningham, husband of Mrs. Alma K. Gross Cunningham, died at his home at 909 South Albemarle street, at 7 a. m. yesterday. He was 77.

He was born in Springettsbury township, son of the late Albert and Ida Diehl Cunningham, and was a retired employe of the Pennsylvania Railroad.

Besides his widow, he is survived be four sons, Spurgeon H. Cunningham, Hellam R. D. 1; Armond A. Cunningham, Hallam; Ruby R. Cunningham, Hanover, and Francis J. Cunningham, 1100 Springdale avenue; three sisters, Mrs. Sarah Keller, Mountville; Mrs. Harry Witmer, York R. D. 9, and Mrs. Frank Henise, 805 Topper street; a brother Raymond, Wrightsville; 26 grandchildren and 23 great-grandchildren.

The Rev. Jerome F. Diehl, Bethany E. U. B. Church, will officiate at funeral services at 2 p. m. Thursday at the Etzweiler Funeral Home, 1111 East Market street. Burial will be in Mt. Zion Cemetery.

90th Birthday

4/8/59 GAZ.

Mrs. Charles Cunningham, 653 West Philadelphia street, observed her 90th birthday on March 22.

A former resident of North Sherman street extended, Pleasureville, Mrs. Cunningham is now residing with her son-in-law and daughter, Mr. and Mrs. C. E. Raffensberger.

Mrs. Cunningham spent her birthday quietly, enjoying the numerous bouquets of flowers and greetings sent to her by friends.

1544

Mrs. Emma L. Cunningham

The funeral of Mrs. Emma L. Cunningham wife of L. D. Cunningham, who died suddenly last Monday was held yesterday afternoon with services at the family residence, 1317 West Philadelphia street, at 1:30 o'clock. Rev. H. T. Bowersox, pastor of St. James' Lutheran church, officiated and was assisted by Rev. Fred Geesey of Spring Grove. The pallbearers were six nephews of the deceased: Samuel Hykes, Harry Hykes, Martin Cunningham, Allen Cunningham, David Hess and George Hess. Interment was made in Greenmount cemetery. 7-18-1919

D15. — 3/12/60

Mrs. Minnie S. Cunningham

Mrs Minnie S. Cunningham, 90, of 653 West Philadelphia street, died at 4:05 a. m. today at York Hospital. She was the widow of Charles Cunningham. 1549

Surviving are two stepdaughters, Mrs. Charles Raffensberger, with whom she resided, and Mrs. Spurgeon Hartman, St. Petersburg, Fla.; a s.epson. Allen D. Cunningham, 39 North Gotwalt street; 16 grandchildren, 32 great-grandchildren, 10 great-great grandchildren, a sister, Mrs. William Lentz, Leader's Heights, and two brothers, Charles S ough, York R. D. 8, and Martin Stough, Seven Vall:ys.

The Rev. J. William Anderson, pastor of Mt. Zion Uni'ed Church of Christ, where Mrs. Cunningham was a member, will conduct the funeral at 2 p. m. Tuesday at the Robert F. Koller Funeral Home, 2000 West Market street. Interment will be in Mt. Zion Cemetery.

1544

Emma C. Cunningham

York 2-5-95 S.N

Emma C. Shermeyer Cunningham of York died at 7:50 p.m. Friday at Manor Care South. She was 91.

Mrs. Cunningham worked as a cook at Yorkview Homes and retired in 1966 as a picker for Tioga Mills. She was a member of Mount Zion Lutheran Church.

Born on Oct. 5, 1903, in Hellam, she was a daughter of the late Frank and Sara J. Strong Shermeyer. She was the wife of the late Jennings B. "Jim" Cunningham.

She leaves four sons, Glenn F. Cunningham, Felton, Merle J. Cunningham and John D. Cunningham, both of York Haven, and Carl E. Cunningham, Seven Valleys; two daughters, Eva A. Arvin, York, and Nancy M. Schrum, Dover; 23 grandchildren; 34 great-grandchildren; several great-great-grandchildren; a brother, William E. Shermeyer, York; and a sister, Edna Hauer, York.

The viewing is from 1:30 to 2 p.m. Tuesday at the Everhart-Jackson-Heffner Funeral Home Inc., 1205 E. Market St., York. The service is at 2 p.m. at the funeral home, with the Rev. Michael Bahn, chaplain of Manor Care South, officiating.

The burial will be in the Mount Zion Cemetery.

Ruth E. Cunningham

1544

MOUNT WOLF — Ruth E. Cunningham, 84, of Mount Wolf, died 2 a.m. Saturday at Memorial Hospital.

The service will be 11 a.m. Tuesday at the L.E. Diehl Funeral Home Inc., 87 S. Main St., Mount Wolf. Burial will be in Mount Zion Cemetery, Springettsbury Township. Viewing will be from 10 to 11 a.m. Tuesday at the funeral home. Memorial contributions may be made to St. John's Lutheran Church, Third and Center sts., Mount Wolf, 17347.

Miss Cunningham was born in Springettsbury Township, near Pleasurerville, the daugher of the late James F. and Elizabeth (Shenberger) Cunningham.

She was a member of St. John Lutheran Church, Mount Wolf. She worked for many years for New York Wire Cloth Company of York, and was the oldest member of its Quarter Century Club.

Surviving are two sisters, Pauline G. Benedict and E. Frances Boll, both of Mount Wolf.

Officiating at the service will be her pastor, the Rev. Bernard F. Engelhardt.

01-27-90

YORK DAILY RECORD

SUNDAY JAN. 28, 1990

1544

Spurgeon Cunningham

HALLAM — Spurgeon H.J. Cunningham Sr., 81, of 28 W. Market St., died Sunday morning at his home. He was the husband of Estella G. (Reever) Cunningham, who died in 1987. He is survived by 20 children, plus 103 other living descendents.

The service will be 10 a.m. Wednesday at the Etzweiler Funeral Home, 1111 E. Market St., York. Burial will be in Mount Zion Cemetery. Viewing will be 7 to 9 p.m. Tuesday at the funeral home. Memorial contributions may be made to American Heart Association, 301 E. Market St., York, 17403; or to Frienship Fire Company, Hallam, 17406.

Mr. Cunningham was born in Springettsbury Township. He was the son of the late Jacob and Alma (Gross) Cunningham.

He retired as a foreman with the New York Wire Cloth Co. in York, where he was employed 45 years. He was a member of Kreutz Creek Valley VFW Post 7045, of Kreutz Creek Valley Ambulance Club, the Hawk Gunning Club, Friendship Fire Company and the Quarter Century Club of New York Wire.

Mr. Cunningham is survived by 11 sons, Preston E. Cunningham, James W. Cunningham, Clarence E. Cunningham, Kenneth R. Cunningham, Blaine R. Cunningham, all of York, Dennis F. Cunningham, Barry L. Cunningham, Alan B. Cunningham and Robert L. Cunningham, all of Wrightsville, Spurgeon H. Cunningham Jr. of Craley, and Mark J. Cunningham of Glendale, Ariz.

Also, nine daughters, June L. Clinton of York, Gladys E. Beck and Alma F. Klahold, both of York RD 11, Patsy J. Heiland of Glendale, Phyllis A. Dellinger of Red Lion, Darlerne M. Cunningham of York, Mary Lou Gross of Mechanicsburg & Judith R. Fourhman of Maryland Line, Md., and Linda K. Willson of Red Lion RD 2.

Also, there ar 54 grandchildren; 47 great-grandchildren; two great-great-granddaughters; three brothers, Armond Cunningham of Hallam, Rudy Cunningham of Hanover, and Francis Cunningham of York.

Officiating at the service will be the Rev. C.W. Willson, a retired United Methodist minister. 07-21-91

York Daily Record Monday July 22, 1991

1544

Estella G. Cunningham: York area native

Mrs. Estella G. Cunningham, 75, York RD 11, died Thursday morning at York Hospital.

She was the wife of Spurgeon H. Cunningham Sr.

Mrs. Cunningham, born in Springettsbury Township, was a daughter of the late Emanuel J. and Flora E. Knaub Reever.

Survivors include:

Eleven sons — Preston E. Cunningham, 4330 Webster Drive; Spurgeon H. Cunningham Jr., Craley; James W. Cunningham, 220 Edgewood Road; Clarence E. Cunningham, York RD 11; Dennis F. Cunningham, 545 W. Princess St.; Kenneth R. Cunningham, 3891 Oakleigh Drive; Blaine R. Cunningham, 735 Priority Road; Barry L. Cunningham, Columbia; Alan B. Cunningham, 407 S. Second St., Wrightsville; Mark J. Cunninghamn, Glendale, Ariz.; and Robert L. Cunningham, 235 Chestnut St., Wrightsville.

Nine daughters — June L. Clinton, 2800 Mt. Rose Ave.; Gladys E. Beck and Alma F. Klahold, both of York RD 11; Patsy J. Heiland, Glendale, Ariz.; Phyllis A. Cunningham, Country Club Road, Red Lion; Darlene M. Cunningham, 909 S. Albemarle St.; Mary Lou Gross, Dillsburg RD 2; Judith R. Fourhman, Maryland Line, Md.; and Linda K. Willson, Red Lion RD 2.

Fifty-four grandchildren and 34 great-grandchildren.

Three brothers — Kenneth E. Reever, York; Leonard J. Reever, Nashville; and Millard F. Reever, York RD 12.

Three sisters — Nettie P. Forry, York; Flossie N. Glatfelter, Red Lion; and Evelyn Waltimeyer, Seattle, Wash.

Viewing will be 7 to 9 p.m. Saturday at the Etzweiler Funeral Home, 1111 E. Market St.

Funeral service will be 2 p.m. Sunday at the funeral home with the Rev. C. Wesley Willson, retired United Methodist minister, officiating.

Memorial contributions may be made to the American Heart Association, York County Council, 320 E. Philadelphia St., York, Pa. 17403.

York Dispatch Friday June 26, 1987

1544

Mrs. Spurgeon W. Cunningham

A private funeral service was

6

Appendices

Legal Documents of William Cunningham Estate

Personal Property Appraisal Documents

These documents relate to the inventory and appraisement of the personal property of William Cunningham, who was from Springettsbury Township in the County of York, Pennsylvania. The document is filed under No. 186 and was filed on October 31st, 1901. It is recorded in Book No. 18 on page 587. The fee of $1.50 has been paid, and the document is signed by an attorney, A.N. Green.

Front Cover:

No. 186

Filed Oct. 31st A. D. ~~189~~1901

William Cunningham

Inventory and Appraisement of the Personal Property of

William Cunningham

late of Springetsbury Township

in the County of York, and State of Pennsylvania, deceased

Recorded in Book No. 18

on page 587 and compared.

Fee $1.50 Paid

A. N. Green,
Attorney.

Inventory and Appraisement Document

State of Pennsylvania,

YORK COUNTY, ss:

Personally came before me a Justice of the Peace in and for said county Ed W Fosche and Martin Sipe who after being duly ~~sworn~~ affirmed according to Law, did say that at the request of Albert Cunningham & David W Cunningham Esq they will well and truly, and without prejudice or partiality, value and appraise the goods and chattels, rights and credits which were of William Cunningham late of Springettsbury Twp York county, Pa., deceased, and in all respects perform their duties as Appraisers, to the best of their skill and judgment.

Affirmed and subscribed to before me this 10th day of August A. D. 1897
Edmund Dietz J P

Ed W Fosche
Martin Sipe

INVENTORY AND APPRAISEMENT

of the good and chattels, rights and credits which were of William Cunningham late of Springettsbury Twp in the County of York taken and made in conformity with the above deposition.

Boards, Barrels, Stove Box & Tobacco lath	4 00
Bed & Spring [illegible]	2 50
Hay	4 00
Pump tools & fixtures	30 00
Barrels Boxes, Trough & frames	3 50
Old lumber, Posts & sled	4 25
Tobacco cutter, Barrels, Box & Hay cutter	3 50
[illegible] Ladder, Logs &c	3 00
Lot of chickens	14 00
5 Hogs @ 6.00 per head	30 00
Feed Box Dipper Iron, Sausage Grinder	3 50
Carpenters Tools	10 00
Amt carried over	112 75

Page 1 Summary:

- Date: August 10, 1897
- Appraisers: Ed W. Loucks and Martin Sipe
- Items Listed: Detailed inventory of goods and chattels, rights, and credits of William Cunningham, including household items, livestock, and tools.

Transcription of the document:

State of Pennsylvania,
YORK COUNTY, SS:

Personally came before me, a Justice of the Peace in and for said county, Ed W. Loucks and Martin Sipe, who, after being duly sworn or affirmed according to law, did say that at the request of the Commonwealth of Pennsylvania, Davis W. Cunningham, Ex., they will well and truly, and without prejudice or partiality, value and appraise the goods and chattels, rights and credits which were of William Cunningham, deceased, late of Springettsbury Twp., York county, Pa., and in all respects perform their duties as Appraisers, to the best of their skill and judgment.

Affirmed and subscribed to before me this 10th day of August, A.D. 1897
Edmund Dietz, J.P.

E. W. Loucks
Martin Sipe

Page 2 with summary:

Amount brought over	112 75
Benches. Lot of Onions, Table & Sundries	4 50
Fire Extinguisher	1 00
Cook Stove	3 00
5 Chairs & Rocker	60
Clock	1 50
Table, Chest, Sink Bench Dishes &	4 50
Looking Glass & Carpet	1 50
Bed, Chest, Desk	4 00
Crocks & 4 Lard cans Lard Press	2 50
Lawn Mower	1 00
Iron Board, Bench Baskets, tin Buckets & Brooms	4 60
Cradle	25
Side Board	2 00
Bed & Bedstead	2 00
Looking Glass	25
Carpet	2 00
Chest	3 00
Bureau	4 00
Lounge	2 50
Chairs Rocker & Stands	1 50
Lot of Carpet & Rugs	9 00
Bed & Bedding	6 00
Bureau Chairs & stand	8 00
3 Guns & Rifle	20 00
8 Blinds	3 00
3 Watches	17 00
Amt	221 75

Continuation of various household items and their corresponding values, written in a cursive script. The list includes furniture, glassware, textiles, and even a rifle.

Here are some specific items mentioned:

* Glassware

* Furniture (including beds, chests, and chairs)

* Rugs

* A rifle

* Possibly household linens or textiles

Final Page with Summary:

Amt brought over	221 75
Spectacles & Razors	1 50
Parlor & ten Plate stoves	6 00
Lot of Dishes	3 00
" " Jars	2 00
4 umbrellas	3 00
Side Board, chairs, Rocker & table	7 15
Clock, Looking Glass, & waiters	3 50
Carpets	14 00
Sewing Machine	1 00
Bureau, Chair Rocker	5 00
Buffet	6 00
Lounge	6 00
Parlor Suit Wheel, Rocker Blinds & Lamp	3 00
Lot of vases	2 00
" " canned fruit	3 00
Lard cans	4 00
Violin	5 00
1 share in gun	5 00
5 Shares Central Market House stock	37 50
Cash	45 00
Prom. Note of Albert Cunningham	21 00
" " " " "	100 00
" " " D W "	97 00
" " " J E "	54 00
Taken and Appraised by us this 1st day of August A.D. 1899.	$ 672 40

Martin Sipe

Items Listed: Continues to list various household items, personal belongings, and their associated values.

- Appraisal Date: August 26, 1899
- Appraiser Signature: Signed by Martin Sipe

Transcription of the document:

Amount brought over—-$221.75

Spectacles & Razors: $1.50
Parlor & tin Plate stoves: $6.00
Lot of Dishes: $3.00
Lot of Iron: $2.00
4 umbrellas: $3.00
Side Board, chair, Rocker & Table: $7.15
Clock, Turkey Floor, 4 waiters: $3.50
Carpets: $14.00
Sewing Machine: $1.00
Bureau, Chair, Rocker: $5.00
Buffet: $6.00
Lounge: $6.00
Parlor Suit, Wheel, Rocker Blinds & Lamp: $23.00
Lot of crocks: $2.00
Lot of canned fruit: $3.00
Lot of corn: $4.00
Violin: $5.00
1 shotgun: $5.00
5 shares Central Market House Stock: $37.50
Cash: $46.00
Promissory Note of Albert Cunningham: $21.00
Promissory Note of Albert Cunningham: $100.00

Promissory Note of Albert Cunningham: $97.00
Promissory Note of Albert Cunningham: $50.00

Total: $672.40

Taken and Appraised by me this 26th day of August A.D. 1899.
Martin Sipe

Detailed Property List Document:

The 29-page document appears to be an itemized list of properties designated to specific individuals, detailing the value of each item in dollars and cents during an estate sale. This comprehensive list is associated with the estate of William Cunningham, Ex-County Commissioner.

Summary of Key Points:

- Document Type: Itemized property list for the estate of William Cunningham
    - Content: Detailed listings of properties, designated individuals, and their respective values
    - Format: Organized in columns with specific values

Front Cover:

(54)
Estate of William Cunningham
deceased, late of Springfield Twp.
Albert Cunningham and
David W. Cunningham
No. 54 Executors
Filed Nov. 4th 1901.
Vendue List

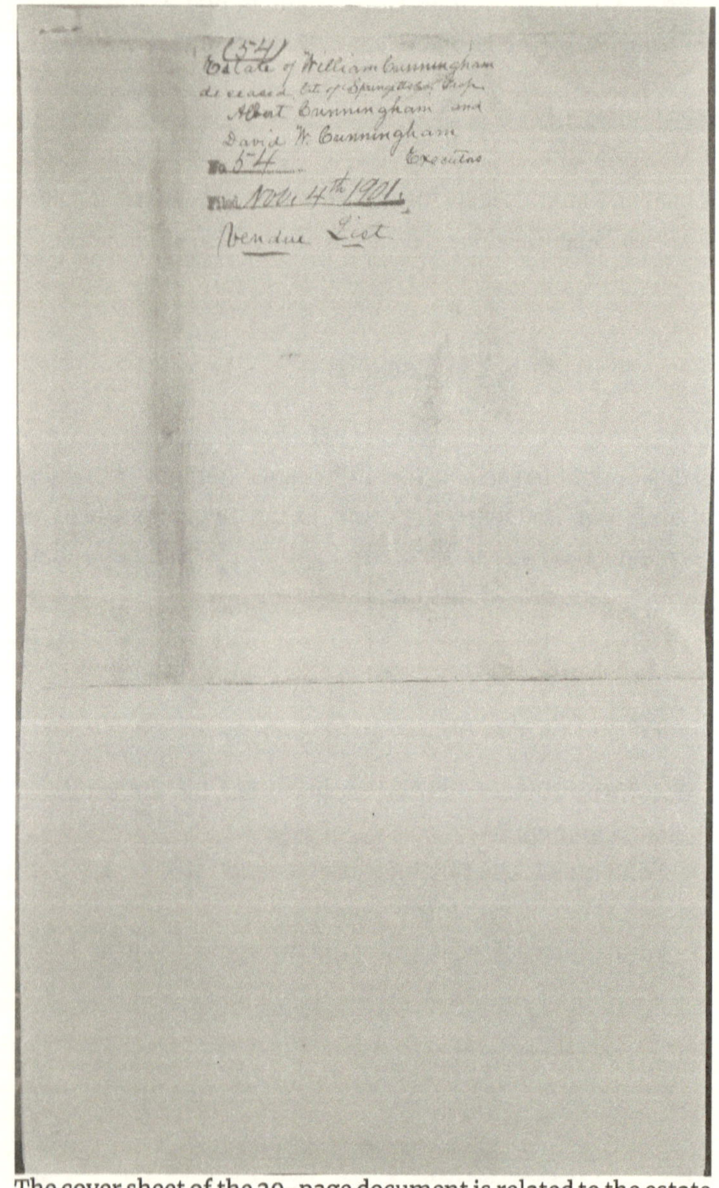

The cover sheet of the 29-page document is related to the estate of William Cunningham, deceased. It mentions the executors Albert Cunningham and David W. Cunningham. The document is officially filed on November 4th, 1901, and it is referred to as the “Vendue List”.

Page 1:

	Names	Articles			
1	Abraham Isaac	Lot of Iron	✓		05
2	" "	[illegible]	✓		01
3	Cunningham Eli	[illegible]	✓		24
4	" "	Lot of Spoons	✓		25
5	Cunningham Albert	Bands & Rings	✓		20
6	" Eli	[illegible]	✓		10
7	" "	Sundries [illegible]	✓		2[illegible]
8	" "	Pump handle	✓		10
9	Abraham Isaac	" "	✓		05
10	Cunningham Albert	[illegible]	✓		05
11	[illegible]	[illegible]	✓		85
12	Cunningham Eli	Sundries	✓		15
13	Cunningham Albert	Hinges & Bands	✓		15
14	" Albert	Bands	✓		10
15	" "	"	✓		20
16	" Eli	"	✓		2[illegible]
17	" Albert	"	✓		15
18	" "	Old Iron	✓		04
19	Abraham Isaac	Lot of Old Iron	✓	1	30
20	Cunningham Eli	Pulley &c	✓		10
21	" Albert	Straw Cutter	✓	1	20
22	" D. H.	Tobacco [illegible]	✓		25
23	Abraham Isaac	[illegible] lock	✓		01
24	" "	[illegible] &c	✓		01
25	[illegible]	[illegible]	✓		01
26	[illegible]	[illegible]	✓		2
				5	20

Page 2:

	Names	Articles		cts
27	Runk Isaac	[illegible]		[illegible]
28	[illegible] Wm	[illegible]	✓	[illegible]
29	Cunningham Eli	[illegible]	✓	[illegible]
30	" "	Chain	✓	[illegible]
31	[illegible] Reuben	[illegible] "	✓	[illegible]
32	[illegible] Wm	[illegible] "	✓	1 [illegible]
33	Cunningham D.W.	Mattock	✓	[illegible]
34	" [illegible]	[illegible]	✓	[illegible]
35	" Eli	"	✓	35
36	[illegible] Wm	Rake &c	✓	05
37	Stevenson [illegible]	Barrel & [illegible]	X	9[illegible]
38	Peters George	[illegible]	✓	[illegible]
39	Cunningham Albert	Lot of Corn	✓	63
40	" D.W.	Lot [illegible]	✓	7 [illegible]
41	" Eli	Lot of [illegible]	✓	[illegible]
42	" "	[illegible]	✓	13
43	[illegible]	[illegible]	✓	[illegible]
44	Cunningham D.W.	Basket Bush[illegible]	✓	20
45	" Eli	[illegible]	✓	[illegible]
46	" "	Tobacco Case	✓	15
47	" "	" "	✓	[illegible]
48	[illegible] John	" "	✓	2[illegible]
49	Rohrbaugh G.W.	Barrel	✓	65
50	Cunningham Eli	Tobacco Case	✓	18
51	Rohrbaugh G.W.	3 [illegible] 2 pip	✓	[illegible]
52	Cunningham Albert	[illegible]	✓	[illegible]
			14	60

Page 3:

	names	articles			Am
53	Richard Mrs Wm	Keg	✓		40
54	Almony Joseph	Ladder	✓	1	75
55	Cunningham, Eli	Tobacco Case	✓		12
56	" Albert	Lot of Lay	✓	7	70
57	" "	Doors No 1	✓		26
58	" Eli	" " 2	✓		15
59	" Albert	" " 3	✓		[illegible]
60	Rinck Isaac	" " 4 (Panel)	✓		35
61	Cunningham Eli	" " 5	✓		35
62	" Albert	" " 6	✓		30
63	Stacks S. H.	" " 7	✓		45
64	Cunningham Albert	[illegible]	✓		03
65	" Eli	Block + Tackle &c Paper	✓		10
66	" "	Lot of Scantling	✓		95
67	" "	" " Strips	✓		15
68	Stack Thomas H	Lot of Lumber	✓		25
69	Cunningham Albert	Lot of Pine flooring	✓		50
70	" Eli	1 Board	✓		33
71	" Albert	Tobacco Bale	✓		35
72	Peters George	4 Boards	✓		33
73	Abraham Isaac	Lot of Parings	✓		30
74	Cunningham Albert	" Ceiling	✓	1	45
75	" D. H.	Stand Bow	✓		11
76	Peters William	Stand Buckets &c	✗		15
77	Nye Wm	Stove Plugs	✓		15
78	Cunningham Albert	Digging Iron	✓		50
				18	00

Page 4:

	Names	articles		cts
79	Cunningham Eli	Wheel [illegible]	✓	[illegible]
80	[illegible] George	Lot of tin [illegible]	✓	[illegible]
81	Cunningham Eli	Lot of [illegible]	✓	3[illegible]
82	Williams George	Harrow	✓	[illegible]
83	Cunningham Albert	Lot of Lumber	✓ 3	[illegible]
84	" Eli	Lot of Palings [illegible]	✓	12
85	Abraham Isaac	Lot of Posts	✓	7[illegible]
86	Cunningham Eli	Cultivator	✓	3[illegible]
87	"	[illegible]	✓	1[illegible]
88	" E. H.	Lot of [illegible]	✓	1[illegible]
89	Abraham Isaac	Pile of [illegible]	✓	1[illegible]
90	" "	Lot of Iron	✓	10
91	[illegible]	Lot of Doors	✓	[illegible]
92	Cunningham Albert	Lot of [illegible]	✓	20
93	Abraham Isaac	Lot of [illegible]	✓	86
94	Cunningham Eli	Lot of Scantling No 1	✓	1[illegible]
95	" Albert	Lot of Boards No 2	✓	30
96	" Eli	" " " 3	✓	2[illegible]
97	"	" " 4	✓	[illegible]
98	" Albert	" " No 5	✓	16
99	"	Hog trough	✓	1[illegible]
100	Miller George [illegible]	Lot of [illegible]	✓	[illegible]
101	[illegible]	[illegible]	✓	[illegible]
102	Cunningham Albert	Lot of [illegible]	✓	2[illegible]
103	Miller H. A.	[illegible]	✓	[illegible]
104	Cunningham Eli	Jack	✓	[illegible]
			8	4[illegible]

Page 5:

	Names	Articles			cts
105	Sipe Martin	[illegible]	✓		04
106	[illegible] Mrs [illegible]	Scalding Trough	✓	2	15
107	Miller Geo H	Lot of [illegible]	✓		20
108	Abraham Isaac	"	✓		25
109	Cunningham Albert	[illegible]	✓		06
110	Eli	Lot of [illegible]	✓		10
111	Abraham Isaac	Table & Doors	✓		15
112	Dehoff [illegible]	[illegible]	✓		10
113	Cunningham Albert	Lot of [illegible]	✓		15
114	" "	Box & Planks	✓		30
115	" Eli	Lot of Boxes	✓		15
116	" "	Lot of [illegible]	✓		02
117	" David	Maple Trough	✓		10
118	Ferree Samuel 6	Hog Gallows	✓		25
119	Cunningham Albert	Lot of Shingles	✓	1	20
120	" "	Halter	✓		15
121	Abraham Isaac	[illegible]	✓		05
122	Cunningham Eli	Lot of [illegible]	✓		10
123	" "	" " "	✓		15
124	Abraham Isaac	[illegible]	✓		05
125	Cunningham Eli	[illegible]	✓		25
126	Loucks Ed H	[illegible]	✓		10
127	Miller Geo H	Lot of Boards	✓		15
128	Kunk Isaac ✗	Grindstone	✗	1	35
129	Abraham Isaac	Couplings	✓		08
130	Cunningham Albert	Lot of Lumber	✓		75
				7	96

Page 6:

	Names	Articles		$	cts
131	Cunningham Eli	Box	✓		01
132	" Albert	Lot of Shingles	✓		21
133	Abraham Isaac	Lot of Lumber	✓	1	00
134	Piff Edward	Axe	✓		15
135	Cunningham Albert	Rake	✓		08
136	[illegible]	Fruit Picker	✓		23
137	Cunningham Eli	Box	✓		02
138	" "	Lot of Lumber	✓		13
139	" "	" "	✓		[illegible]
140	" Albert	" " "	✓		45
141	Myers J. C.	Wood [illegible] Boiler	✓		10
142	Abraham Isaac	Stove pipe &c	✓		21
143	Peters Geo B.	Drying Iron	✓		60
144	Abraham Isaac	Cigar Moulds	✓		01
145	Cunningham Albert	Dryer &c pans	✓		08
146	" "	Sundries Bot [illegible]	✓		01
147	" "	Bevel	✓		02
148	" Eli	Lot of papers Box	✓		03
149	" "	" " Boxes	✓		08
150	[illegible]	Wine press	✓		11
151	Cunningham Albert	Drying Board	✓		02
152	Abraham Isaac	Lot of [illegible] &c	✓		01
153	Miller Geo W.	Lot of [illegible] &c	✓	1	20
154	Cunningham J. P.	Barrels [illegible]	✓	2	10
155	Richards Wm	Lot of [illegible]	✓		65
156	Cunningham D. W.	Lot of [illegible]	✓		10
				7	91

Page 7:

	Names	articles	cts
157	Miller Geo. W.	Lot of [illegible]	1 04
158	[illegible]	[illegible] Tube	06
159	Cunningham [illegible]	[illegible]	[illegible]
160	" Albert	Boards	[illegible]
161	Piff Edward	Sieve (ash)	02
162	Cunningham Eli	[illegible]	[illegible]
163	Wherley Geo.	Wire netting	13
164	Sipe [illegible]	Clover seed	10
165	Schake Wm.	Snow Shovel	08
166	Shultz Henry	" "	13
167	Cunningham D. H.	Pail	06
168	[illegible]	[illegible]	10
169	Wherley Geo.	Sausage Grinder	66
170	Cunningham [illegible]	Canteen [illegible]	01
171	Sipe [illegible]	[illegible]	[illegible]
172	[illegible]	[illegible]	03
173	Cunningham Albert	[illegible]	02
174	" "	[illegible]	01
175	Piff Edward	2 Wedges	[illegible]
176	Wherley Geo.	[illegible]	[illegible]
177	Cunningham Albert	Pair [illegible]	02
178		[illegible]	01
179	[illegible]	[illegible]	02
180	[illegible]	Oil cans	01
181	Cunningham Eli	Box [illegible]	[illegible]
182	[illegible]son Wm. X	[illegible] X	10
			2 64

Page 8:

	Names	Articles		
83	Runk Isaac	Rakes	✓	02
84	Stambaugh C. F.	Forks	✓	02
85	Sipe J. S.	Lot of Ware	✓	11
86	Cunningham David	Carpet & bags &c	✓	12
87	Sipe J. S.	Loop Iron Auger &c	✓	05
188	Rohrbaugh Geo	Hay Knife	✓	15
189	Zech Wm.	Pumps	✓	35
190	Cunningham Eli	Lot of Sundries	✓	34
191	Freyd Jacob Jr	Lot of gun stalks	✓	09
192	Poff Edward	Shovel &c	✓	02
193	Cunningham Eli	Lot of sundries	✓	01
194	Spangler Alex	Corn Hoppers	✓	07
195	Leckrone H. J.	" "	✓	02
196	Stambaugh C. F.	Lot of Screws	✓	03
197	Loucks Edw	Oil cloth	✓	05
198	Sipe J. S.	Lot of Flax &c	✓	16
199	Frey Wm.	Salt &c	✓	15
200	Cunningham Eli	Water can &c	✓	01
201	Cunningham David	Lard Stone &c	✓	01
202	Frey Wm.	Kettle &c	✓	23
203	Cunningham Eli	Pump Spouts	✓	13
204	Sipe Martin	Lot of ware	✓	02
205	Zech Adam	2 Barrels	✓	39
206	Stebel Charles A.	Line Box	✓	11
207	Miller H. A.	Lot of Bags	✓	06
208	" "	Oil Cloth &c	✓	01
				233

Page 9:

	names	articles	$	cts
209	Stevenson William	[illegible]		18
210	Miller H. A.	Bag & [illegible]		03
211	" "	Lot of Bags		10
212	[illegible] M. S.	Cheese Box &c		65
213	Cunningham Eli	Lot of sundries		01
214	" D. H.	Tool Chest		50
215	" Eli	Box & Red paint		35
216	Runk Isaac	2 Boxes paint		39
217	Cunningham Albert	Paint Buckets		[illegible]
218	" "	"		20
219	Miller H. A.	" "		02
220	Cunningham [illegible]	Paint & [illegible]		[illegible]
221	" "	" Baskets		15
222	" Albert	Box & lime		11
223	" "	Barrel & [illegible]		35
224	Miller H. A.	[illegible]		07
225	[illegible]	[illegible]		38
226	[illegible]	Gallon measure		26
227	Chester Jacob	3 rods & [illegible]	1	05
228	Myers G. C.	Tree Trimmer		10
229	Cunningham David	[illegible] Bits		02
230	Chester Jacob	" Bit		04
231	" "	" "		06
232	Cunningham David	" "		01
233	" "	" "		01
234	" "	" "		01
			3	36

Page 10:

	Names	Articles	$	cts
			✓	01
235	Cunningham [illegible]	Pump [illegible]	✓	01
236	" "	" "	✓	11
237	" "	" "	✓	11
238	" Eli	" "	✓	05
239	Rhodes Jacob	" "	✓ 1	10
240	"	" "	✓	70
241	Cunningham Eli	Ladle	✓	01
242	" Albert	20 Chickens @ 30	✓ 6	00
243	" "	35 [illegible] @ 21	✓ 7	35
244	" D. H.	Kettle Stand	✓	30
245	Lecktrone H. J.	" "	✓	45
246	[illegible] Wm	[illegible]	✓	40
247	Stambaugh C. F.	[illegible]	✓	07
248	DeHoff Reuben	Hammer	✓	01
249	Cunningham D. H.	Corn Basket	✓	15
250	" "	Iron Kettle	✓ 6	60
251	[illegible] Morris (Amy)	"	✓ 2	50
252	Lecktrone H. J.	2 [illegible] @ 2	✓	04
253	Cunningham Albert	2 [illegible] @ 05	✓	10
254	Stauffer Harry	Saw [illegible]	✓	25
255	Myers J. C.	[illegible]	✓	40
256	Stevenson Wm	2 Augers	✓	[illegible]
257	Cunningham Eli	1 Auger	✓	10
258	Stevenson William	" "	✓	4
259	Cunningham Albert	" "	✓	26
260	DeHoff Reuben	2 Augers @ 6	✓	12
			23	02

Page 11:

	Names		Articles		$	cts
261	Frey Wm		1 Auger	✓		30
262	[illegible] Wm		" "	✓		45
263	Cunningham Albert		" "	✓		31
264	Frey William		2 "	✓		32
265	Cunningham Albert		Coffee kettle	✓	6	10
266	[illegible]	X	Plane	X		20
267	Frye Joseph		"	✓		15
268	[illegible]		[illegible] Plane	✓		[illegible]
269	[illegible]		"	✓		06
270	Shaffer [illegible]		Plane	✓		[illegible]
271	[illegible]		Lot of Planes	✓		01
272	[illegible]		"	✓		10
273	Frey [illegible]		[illegible]	✓		[illegible]
274	[illegible]		Lot of planes	✓		07
275	Frey [illegible]		[illegible]	✓		19
276	Spangler [illegible]		Drawing Knife	✓		21
277	[illegible]		[illegible]	✓		30
278	Spangler J. S.		Plane	✓		03
279	Spangler Benjamin		[illegible]	✓		30
280	Snyder C. B.		Wrench & hammer	✓		[illegible]
281	Cunningham [illegible]		Files	✓		[illegible]
282	" William		2 [illegible] planes @ [illegible]	✓	1	[illegible]
283	" Eli		2 chisels @ [illegible]	✓		20
284	Bahn Franklin		2 [illegible] @ [illegible]	✓		15
285	Peters Wm	X	Pinchers	X		06
286	Cunningham [illegible]		2 "	✓		[illegible]
					12	10

Page 12:

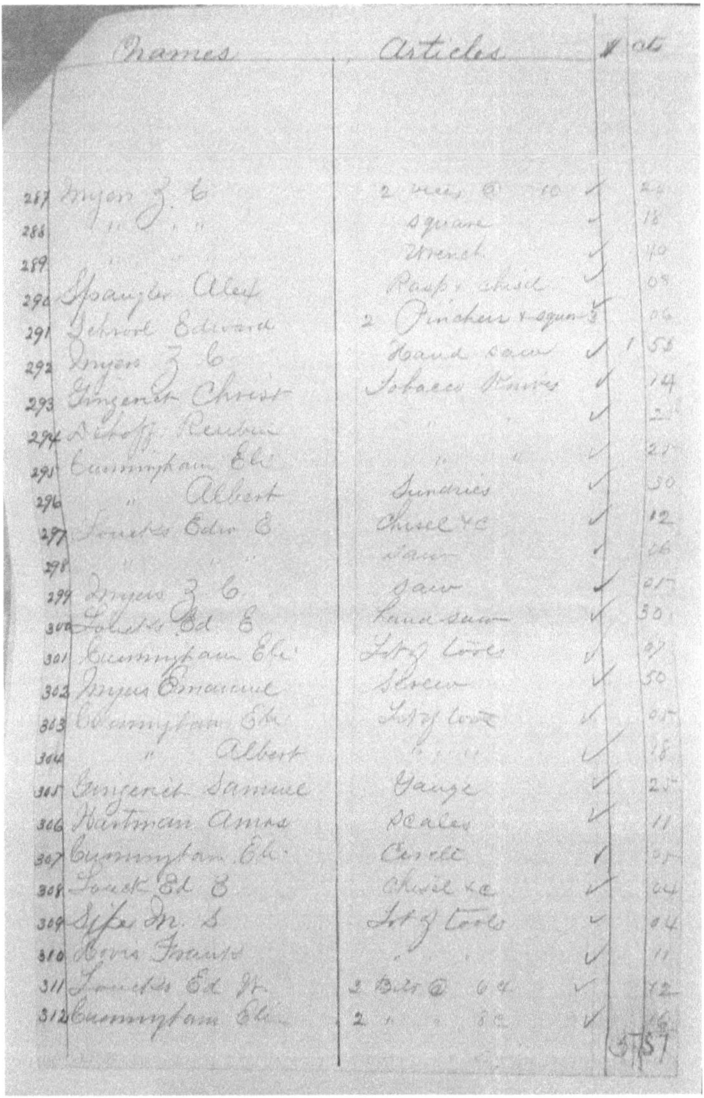

	Names	Articles		$	cts
287	Myers Z. C.	2 vices @ 10	✓		20
288	" " "	square	✓		18
289	" " "	Wrench	✓		10
290	Spangler Aleck	Rasp & chisel	✓		08
291	Schrock Edward	2 Pinchers & square	✓		06
292	Myers Z. C.	Hand saw	✓	1	55
293	Gingerich Christ	Tobacco Knives	✓		14
294	Detoff Reuben	" "	✓		2[illegible]
295	Cunningham Eli	" "	✓		25
296	" Albert	Sundries	✓		30
297	Fouchs Edw E	Chisel &c	✓		12
298	" " "	Saw	✓		06
299	Myers Z. C.	saw	✓		05
300	Fouchs Ed E	hand saw	✓		30
301	Cunningham Eli	Lot of tools	✓		07
302	Myers Emmanuel	Stove	✓		50
303	Cunningham Eli	Lot of tools	✓		05
304	" Albert	" " "	✓		18
305	Gingerich Samuel	Gauge	✓		25
306	Hartman Amos	Scales	✓		11
307	Cunningham Eli	Circle	✓		05
308	Fouch Ed E	Chisel &c	✓		04
309	Sipe M. S	Lot of tools	✓		04
310	Moris Frantz	" "	✓		11
311	Fouchs Ed Jr	2 Bits @ 6¢	✓		12
312	Cunningham Eli	2 " " 8¢	✓		16
				5	57

Page 13:

	Names	Articles	$	ct
313	[illegible]	2 Bits @ [illegible]	✓	[illegible]
314		2 [illegible]	✓	[illegible]
315		[illegible]	✓	[illegible]
316	Cunningham Eli	[illegible]	✓	[illegible]
317	" J E	" " "	✓	[illegible]
318	[illegible] Henry		✓	27
319	[illegible] Edwin	"	✓	[illegible]
320	Cunningham Eli	"	✓	[illegible]
321	[illegible]	2 [illegible] @ 11	✓	[illegible]
322	Cunningham Eli	Lot of Sundries	✓	[illegible]
323	[illegible]	[illegible]	✓	[illegible]
324	[illegible]	[illegible]	✓	[illegible]
325	[illegible]	[illegible]	✓	[illegible]
326	Cunningham Eli	[illegible]	✓	[illegible]
327	[illegible]	[illegible]	✓	[illegible]
328	[illegible]	[illegible]	✓	[illegible]
329	Cunningham Eli	[illegible]	✓	[illegible]
330	"	[illegible]	✓	[illegible]
331	[illegible]	2 Oil [illegible] @ [illegible]	✓	[illegible]
332	Cunningham Albert	Oil stone	✓	[illegible]
333	Miller W. A.	[illegible]	✓	[illegible]
334	Cunningham Albert		✓	[illegible]
335	[illegible] ×	Wallet	×	[illegible]
336	[illegible]	[illegible]	✓	[illegible]
337	[illegible] Henry	[illegible]	✓	[illegible]
338	Cunningham [illegible]	Sundries	✓	[illegible]
			3	[illegible]

Page 14:

	Names	Articles	✓	$	cts
339	Cunningham Eli	Box	✓		01
340	" J. H.	Border flask	✓		01
341	Spangler Emanuel	[illegible]	✓		01
342	Cunningham Albert	Box & sundries			01
343	Lecktrone H. J.	[illegible]	✓		09
344	Hess Samuel F.	Lot of tools	✓		01
345	Cunningham Eli	Box & sundries	✓		04
346	Kostman Amos	Lot of tools	✓		01
347	Cunningham J. E.	Lot of Slot	✓		17
348	"	" " Hedes	✓		20
349	"	Nails	✓		12
350	Miller H. E.	Rope	✓		17
351	Cunningham Eli	Box & putty	✓		12
352	" Albert	Sausage Cutter	✓	2	60
353	" Eli	Screw &c	✓		85
354	Louks Ed. W.	Canvass	✓		80
355	Spangler Benjamin	Adz	✓		06
356	Brenner Henry	Axe	✓		55
357	Frey Henry	Hammer	✓		20
358	Steinbaugh C. F.	Leather	✓	1	55
359	Louks Ed. W.	Soda	✓		20
360	Spangler Albert	Jar & basin	✓		01
361	Mrs Heidlebaugh Aly	Keg & [illegible]	X		02
362	Dellinger George X	Broad axe	X		90
363	Frey Hen	" "	✓	1	15
364	Gingerich David	Post axe	✓		65
				9	61

Page 15:

No.	Name	Item		Amount
365	Cunningham Albert	Dog Iron	✓	10
366	Grim J L	Scale	✓	12
367	Gingerich David	Dog Iron	✓	35
368	Poff Edward	Hand saw	✓	25
369	Cunningham D. W.	Saw	✓	50
370	" Albert	Lot of sundries	✓	20
371	Schroll Edwin	Square	✓	25
372	Cunningham D. W.	Lamp &c	✓	25
373	" Eli	Cow chain	✓	02
374	" "	Post chain	✓	05
375	" Albert	Pot rack	✓	10
376	" Eli	Washline & can	✓	01
377	Poff Edward	Auger	✓	14
378	Cunningham David	Shaft saddle	✓	90
379	Peters William X	Line	✓	95
380	Cunningham Eli	Sundries	✓	01
381	" "	"	✓	01
382	Stevenson Wm	Keg	✓	10
383	Sipe J. S.	Rope & grease	✓	05
384	Snyder C. B.	Lot of rods	✓	15
385	Miller Wm (Auct)	Hackle & hemp	✓	03
386	Spangler Albert	Dustpan &c	✓	10
387	Dietz Frank B. X	Bucket & hammer	X	23
388	Harris Franklin	Lot of bottles	✓	01
389	Cunningham Eli	Pump chain	✓	60
390	" "	Pelter	✓	65
391	Harris Franklin	Can Powder	✓	38
392	Cunningham Eli	Sundries	✓	01
				5 85

Page 16:

394	Cunningham Eli	Box & sundries	✓	18
395	" Albert	Lot of "	✓	25
395	Lefe Fred E.	" " "	✓	15
396	Lestrone Henry J.	Lot of Cans	✓	02
397	Cunningham Eli	" " Cans	✓	01
398	Piff Edward	Lot of Cans	✓	12
399	Cunningham Eli	Can & Oil	✓	65
400	" Albert	Box & sundries	✓	12
401	Immers Amos	Lot of spikes	✓	06
402	Williams George X	Bell & Rack	X	06
403	Cunningham Eli	Box & sundries	✓	03
404	Stambaugh C. F.	Stone & Irons	✓	15
405	Cunningham J. E.	Box & sundries	✓	06
406	Miller Wm (Aust)	Tackle	✓	01
407	Frey Wm	Fire Extinguisher	✓	30
408	Cunningham Eli	Lot of Tools	✓	03
409	" "	Lot of Emery	✓	01
410	" Albert	Register	✓	04
411	" Eli	Trap	✓	01
412	Lestrone H. J.	Box & sundries	✓	02
413	Cunningham J. E.	Oil skins &c	✓	02
414	" D. W.	Black wood	✓	10
415	" Eli	Rasin &c	✓	11
416	" David	Mouse trap	✓	01
417	" D. W.	33 lb Soap @ 4¢	✓	1 32
418	Immers Amos	25 " " " 4¢	✓	1 00
419	Cunningham Albert	33 " " " 3¢	✓	99
	Runtz Isaac X	43 " " 2½¢	X	1 08
				6 67

Page 17:

No.	Name	Article	Amount
421	Dietz W. E. X	Set of soap X	25
422	Sipe Martin	Wash Boiler	10
423	Heiland Moses B.	Oil can	09
424	Loucks Edw W	Onions	38
425	Miller Wm (Auct)	"	25
426	Cunningham Albert	Seed Onions	65
427	Loucks Edw W.	Onions	35
428	" " "	"	38
429	Kindig John Mrs X	Lot of crocks &c X	21
430	Cunningham Eli	Peck measure	05
431	Heiland Moses B	Basket	27
432	Leckrone H. J.	"	05
433	Hess Saml F	½ Bush measure	28
434	" " "	Coal Bucket &c	06
435	Cunningham Eli	Varnish	01
436	Cunningham Wm	Hunters coat	1 10
437	" Albert	Timothy seed	10
438	Myers Z. E.	Tape measure	80
439	Cunningham Eli	Rabbits &c	01
440	Freed Jacob J. +	Sundries X	01
441	Frey Wm	Stove & pipe	1 00
442	Cunningham Albert	Table	1 15
443	" "	Work Bench	30
444	Strong Mrs Frank	Meat Bench	33
445	Poff Edward	1 Shoat @ 9½	9 50
446	Kinkle John	2 Shoat @ 8.00	16 00
447	Frey Wm	2 Shoats @ 8.10	16 20
			49 83

Page 18:

No.	Name		Item		Amount
44[illegible]	Zech Adam		Tea Box	✓	60
449	Cunningham Eli		Slop Barrel	✓	05
4[illegible]	Heiland Moses B.		Tool Box	✓	70
4[illegible]	" "		Butter churn	✓	90
452	Foose M. A.		Wash tub	✓	03
453	Cunningham Albert		Stone Jar	✓	08
454	Zech Adam		" "	✓	11
455	Kunkle Henry		" "	✓	40
456	Bahn Franklin		Lot of Jars	✓	10
457	Heiland Moses B		35 lbs Lard @ 8c	✓	2 80
458	Cunningham David		Lot of Jars	✓	02
459	Sprangle Ezra		6 Crocks @ 7½c	✓	45
460	Foose Jr.		6 " " 7c	✓	42
461	Dillinger Henry		6 " " 7c	✓	42
462	Williams Mary		6 " " 7c	✓	42
463	Cunningham Albert		6 " " 3c	✓	18
464	Zech Adam		6 " " 3c	✓	18
465	Cunningham Albert		6 " 2c	✓	12
466	Grim J. L.		2 Jelly crocks @ 3	✓	06
467	Heidlebaugh Alef	X	Fruit cans	✓	03
468	Cunningham D. W.		Scales	✓	30
469	Jahs E. A.	X	2 [illegible] @ 20	X	40
470	Cunningham D. W.		Wash Tub	✓	70
471	Brenner Henry		3 Flat Irons @ 20c	✓	60
472	Gongwer Christ		Pot Lids	✓	04
473	Cunningham J. E.		Wash Board	✓	15
474	" Eli		Butter Churn	✓	05
	" Albert		Lawn Mower	✓	[illegible]

Page 19:

19

No.	Name	Item	Amount
476	Heidlebaugh Alex	Slop bucket	10
477	Richard Fred.	X Bench X	23
478	Cunningham Albert	"	11
479	Thorley George	Table	50
480	Peters William	X Dresser X	25
481	Cunningham David	Chair	03
482	Leckrone H. J.	Bench	05
483	Inners Amos.	Meat Bench	35
484	Hess Sam Sr	Corner Cupboard	05
485	Myers Charles	Dough tray	05
486	Shermyer John C	Barrel	1 40
487	Cunningham Eli	Tub & board	02
488	Spangler Alex	Tub	22
489	Zeck Adam	"	05
490	Cunningham Albert	Sack of flour	25
491	Shermyer John	Sewing Machine	90
492	Cunningham Albert	Barrel & [illegible]	10
493	" "	" & flour	10
494	Peters George	Slaw Cutter	13
495	Gingerich Christian	Spoon &c	01
496	Freed Jacob J.	X 2 Boxes @ 6¢ X	12
497	Cunningham Albert	Dish &c	12
498	Stelt Jacob	X Milk [illegible] X	10
499	Peters George	Brush &c	13
500	Hoffman John Mrs	Cups & saucers	14
501	Cunningham D W	Roaster	73
502	Stelt Zach	2 pans @ 4¢	08
	"	Pan	06
			6 37

Page 20:

20

No.	Name		Item		Amount
504	Dietz W. E.	X	[illegible] @ [illegible]	X	12
505	Kauffman Gilbert		Bucket	✓	10
506	Bowers A. J.	X	2 pans @ [illegible]	X	11
507	Kohr Lewis	X	Iron pot	X	22
508	Spangler Albert		Dish pan	✓	10
509	Cunningham [illegible]		Dishes	✓	03
510	Hess S. F.		Pan	✓	03
511	Brenner Henry		Skillet	✓	36
512	Cunningham Eli Mrs		Bake board	✓	23
513	Kauffman Gilbert		Dutch Oven	✓	30
514	Hess S. F.		½ doz cups & saucers	✓	20
515	Cunningham David		6 Soup plates @ 4c	✓	24
516	Williams Mary		2 dishes @ 11c	✓	22
517	Frose Mr. C.		Knives & forks	✓	16
518	Thorley George		" " "	✓	05
519	Cunningham D. [illegible]		Knives	✓	30
520	Frey Charles	X	Dippers &c	X	10
521	Hess S. F.		Shears [illegible]	✓	13
522	[illegible]		6 plates @ 3c	✓	18
523	Beaverson Mrs Israel		plates & cups	✓	13
524	Dietz W. E.	X	Bag & [illegible]	X	50
525	Zech Adam		2 Bowls @ 6½	✓	13
526	Richard Wm.		Lot of Dishes	✓	02
527	Blum Augustus Mrs	X	[illegible] plates	X	03
529	Cunningham J. E.		Plate	✓	01
[illegible]	Spangler [illegible]		[illegible]	✓	10
					4 63

Page 21:

21

No.	Name		Article			Amount
531	[illegible]		Set of plates	✓		02
532	Leatrone H. J.		Buck &c	✓		02
533	" "		Mirror	✓		50
534	Miller H. C.		Dish	✓		10
535	Brenner Henry J.		Lamps	✓		20
536	Poff Edward		Clock	✓	2	10
537	Cunningham J. E.		Pans	✓		01
538	" D. H.		Lantern	✓		50
539	Wherley George		Board	✓		06
540	Spangler William		4 chairs @ 10	✓		40
541	Cunningham J. E.		Stove	✓		26
542	[illegible]		[illegible]	✓		[illegible]
543	Cunningham J. P.		[illegible]	✓		50
544	Williams George	X	[illegible]	X	1	[illegible]
545	Cunningham J. P.		[illegible]	✓	2	00
546	" Albert		Bed & bedding			50
547	Spangler [illegible]		6 plates @ 3c	✓		18
548	Baum Franklin		6 jars @ 3½	✓		21
549	Hiddlebaugh Alex		6 " @ 3½	✓		21
550	[illegible] Samuel	X	6 " @ 3	X		18
551	Cunningham Albert		6 " @ 3½	✓		21
552	Baer Wm		6 " @ 3	✓		18
553	Cunningham D. H.		4 " @ 3	✓		12
554	Snyder Chas. B.	X	6 " @ 6	X		36
555	Cunningham Albert		6 " [illegible]	✓		[illegible]
	Snyder Chas. B.	X	" " 4c	X		16
					10	06

Page 22:

No.	Name		Item		Amount
557	Cunningham Wm		Shot Gun	✓	11.00
558	Ingers Steward	X	Rifle	X	6.00
559	Miller H A		Shot Gun	✓	1.70
560	Ingers J. C.		Breech Loading gun	✓	20.00
561	" "		Gun bag	✓	2.75
562	Kindig John Wm		2 dishes @ 9c	✓	18
563	Lefever Leander		6 plates @ 8c	✓	48
564	Cunningham Albert		plate	✓	05
565	" "		3 plates @ 2c	✓	06
566	" D. H.		5 cups @ 3c	✓	15
567	Hartman Amos		pitcher	✓	05
568	Kinkle Henry		"	✓	31
569	Cunningham Albert		"	✓	15
570	Hess S. F.	X	[illegible]	X	[illegible]
571	[illegible]		"	✓	[illegible]
572	Hess S. F.	X	Tea Pot	X	02
573	Cunningham D. H.		pitcher	✓	[illegible]
574	Hartman Amos		Bowl	✓	[illegible]
575	Cunningham Albert		glasses	✓	35
576	"		Dish	✓	40
577	Miller H. W.		Box	✓	06
578	Cunningham Charlie		Bowl	✓	02
579	Inners [illegible]		"	✓	[illegible]
580	Miller H. A.		Dish	✓	36
581	Lefever Charles		Lamp	✓	[illegible]
582	Miller H. A.		[illegible]	✓	10
[illegible]	Cunningham Albert		6 tubbs @ 2c	✓	[illegible]
					44.87

Page 23:

23 | 13

No.	Name	Item			Amount
584	Cunningham Jas.	Tumbler	✓		03
585	" Albert	"	✓		02
586	"	4 " @ 4 ¢	✓		16
587	" Charles	3 " @ 3 c	✓		09
588	" D. W.	Gun scab	✓		10
589	" Charles	3 Tumbler @ 6	✓		18
590	Leetsome H. J.	Lot of glassware	✓		05
591	Cunningham Albert	2 Tumbler @ 2½	✓		05
592	Bremner H. J.	3 " " 2¢	✓		06
593	Cunningham D. W.	2 " " 3¢	✓		06
594	" Albert	3 " @ 3½	✓		11
595	Cunningham Jhw	Violin	✓	12	00
596	" Eli	1/6 Interest of Gun	✓	3	00
597	" Charles	Glass Jar	✓		15
598	" Albert	cream mug	✓		05
599	Kindig John Mrs	Spoon holder	✓		02
600	Henry Mrs	Soda Box	✓		04
601	Lefever Mrs Leander ✓	Work Basket	✓		30
602	Stuckler Mrs	Lamp	✓		14
603	" "	"	✓		15
604	Cunningham D. W.	2 vases @ 3¢	✓		06
605	Robb Georgia	2 " " 10c	✓		20
606	Bremner H. J.	1 vase	✓		06
607	Cunningham Albert	2 vases @ 22½	✓		45
608	" D. W.	2 plates @ 6c	✓		12
609	Grim J. L.	Crock	✓		02
610	Hively Slater	Shell [illegible]	✓		08
611	Grim J. L.	Broom	✓		06
				17	61

Page 24:

24 14

No.	Name		Item		Amount
612	Cunningham Albert		Lot of Spoons	✓	12
613	Keener Frank		" " [illegible]	✓	65
614	Foose Wm		" of Spoons	✓	05
615	Sherringer John E.	X	6 Spoons	X	08
616	Horner Frank		Lot of Spoons	✓	13
617	Cunningham D. W.		Coffee Pot	✓	30
618	Stevenson Wm		Basket	✓	20
619	Cunningham Albert		"	✓	[illegible]
620	Peters George		"	✓	32
621	Harland Mame B.		"	✓	4[illegible]
622	Cunningham Albert		"	✓	31
623	Kauffman Gilbert		"	✓	12
624	Harland Mame B.		"	✓	32
625	Sherringer John E.	X	Basket & corks	X	09
626	Cunningham David		Clothes Basket	✓	55
627	Kauffman Gilbert		"	✓	40
628	Cunningham D. W.		Tray	✓	75
629	Geisler Wm	X	Brass Kettle	X	90
630	Kauffman Gilbert		Basket	✓	[illegible]
631	Hartman Anna		Baskets	✓	[illegible]
632	Spangler Wesley	X	Funnel &c.	X	02
633	Ferre Samuel E.		Tinware	✓	32
634	Kauffman Gilbert		Spoons & Ladle	✓	35
	Stumbley [illegible]		Funnel &c.	✓	08
	Heidlebaugh Alex		Basket	✓	0[illegible]
	Cunningham [illegible]		Basket	✓	05
	Miller H. A.		"	✓	03
	Heidlebaugh Alex		"	✓	[illegible]
	[illegible]	X	"	X	[illegible]
					[illegible]

Page 25:

25

Name	Item		Amount
Leckrone H J	Cullinger	✓	04
Foose Mrs	Dish Pan	✓	07
Cunningham J E	Dishes &c	✓	02
Frey Charles	"	✓	02
Ishers Amos	Tea Kettle	✓	37
Cunningham Albert	Buckets	✓	07
Ferre Sam C	Dishes	✓	03
Stevenson Wm	Coffee Pot	✓	05
Cunningham Albert	Cheese Press	✓	10
Henry Mrs	Cake Griddle	✓	06
Horris Frank	Dust Brush	✓	10
Cunningham Albert	3 Jars & churns @ 4	✓	12
" D W	1 "	✓	07
" " "	2 " @ 5¢	✓	10
Miller Mrs	2 Jars @ 4¢	✓	08
Cunningham Albert	2 " @ 4¢	✓	08
Peters Geo	2 " @ 4¢	✓	08
Cunningham David	2 " @ 3¢	✓	06
" D W	2 " @ 5¢	✓	10
" " "	3 " @ 5¢	✓	15
Strickler Mrs	2 " @ 10¢	✓	20
Cunningham Albert	1 " @	✓	05
Miller Mrs	1 "	✓	04
Sipe Martin	1 "	✓	04
Frothe Mrs	1 "	✓	05
Cunningham D W	1 "	✓	07
Lefever Charles	Umbrella	✓	1 00
Fick Adam	"	✓	25
			4 17

Page 26:

26 | | | 12

Name	Item		Amount
Zech Adam	Umbrella	✓	1 10
Lonecke Ed W.	"	✓	1 05
Strickler Mrs.	Lard Press	✓	1 00
Cunningham David	2 Lard cans @ 12	✓	24
Miller Mrs	Lard can	✓	12
Spangler Ezra	Lard can	✓	20
Spangler Alfred	" "	✓	20
Spangler Ezra	" "	✓	18
Goose Mr [illegible]	5 chairs @ 25	✓	1 25
" "	2 Brooms @ 25	✓	50
Hively Edwin X	2 " @ 25	X	50
Cunningham David	2 " " 26	✓	52
" Albert	2 " " 26	✓	52
Strickler Mrs	6 Chairs @ 40	✓	[illegible] 40
Cunningham D. W.	Table cloth	✓	25
" David	" "	✓	35
[illegible] Mrs	" "	✓	31
Lindsey John X	" "	X	26
Harris Frank	Cloth	✓	11
Cunningham Albert	2 [illegible] @ 5	✓	10
Grothe Mrs	Pillow shams	✓	12
Hess S. F.	[illegible]	✓	15
Grothe Mrs	"	✓	10
Cunningham D. W.	Cushion	✓	80
Spangler Clayton X	"	X	75
Lefever Charlie	2 Towels @ 15	✓	30
Grothe Mrs	Blanket	✓	1 00
Cunningham Mrs	2 Blankets @ 60	✓	1 20
			15 08

Page 27:

Name	Item	Amount
Spangler [illegible]	Bureau	2 [illegible]
Hobbs Frank	Buffet	11 50
Foose Mr	Lounge	4 60
Cunningham [illegible]	[illegible]	7 50
" D. H.	3 Chairs @ 25	75
Diehl Jacob	Parlor Suit	36 00
Cunningham [illegible]	Rocker	6 75
" Albert	Tidy	25
Forbes Edward	Wheel	5 00
Cunningham D H	Stand	75
Spangler Clayton x	Cloth	40
Cunningham J. P.	3 Chairs @ 27	81
" " "	Rocker	60
" " "	Chair @ 25	25
" David	Dresser	5 50
Bingaman Samuel x	Stand	90
Cunningham J. P.	Bed & Bedding	6 50
Cunningham David	Rags & Stand	3 00
" Albert 25	[illegible]	20
Whorley George x	Bed	3 75
Cunningham David	Bureau	6 75
Foose Mr	4 Chairs 25	1 00
Myers Charles	Bed & Bedding	5 00
Cunningham J P	Chest	3 50
Foose Mr	Buffet	1 75
Bahr Franklin	Bed & Bedding	7 00
Cunningham Albert	Rocker	25
" J P	Mirror	50
" Albert	4 Chairs @ 15	60
"	Bench	25
		128 81

Page 28:

Name	Item		Amount
Cunningham David	Blanket	✓	[illegible]
" J. P.	Spread	✓	[illegible]
" Albert	[illegible]	✓	[illegible]
[illegible]	"	✗	[illegible]
Cunningham Albert	Rug	✓	[illegible]
" D. W.	2 " [illegible]	✓	10
" Albert	Rug	✓	15
" D. W.	[illegible] goods	✓	10
Grothe Mrs	Netting	✓	15
Zeller Wm (Clerk)	"	✓	45
Spangler Emanuel	[illegible]	✗	30
[illegible] Harry	[illegible]	✗	1 00
[illegible] Ed W.	[illegible]	✓	01
" "	Childs cradle	✓	25
Sipe Alex	Iron Stand	✗	15
Cunningham Albert	Rug	✓	1 30
[illegible] Frank	"	✓	1 00
[illegible]	"	✗	1 32
[illegible] Edw W.	"	✓	90
[illegible] Amos	"	✓	12
Freed Jacob J	Flax	✗	16
Foose Mr	14 yds carpet @ 21c	✓	2 94
Cunningham David	22 " " @ 39c	✓	8 58
" D. W.	20 " " @ 35c	✓	7 00
[illegible] Moses B.	20 " " @ 41	✓	8 20
Cunningham J. E.	20 " " @ 41	✓	8 20
" " "	25 " " @ 38	✓	9 50
Peters George	12½ " @ 25	✓	3 13
Cunningham Albert	8½ @ 10	✓	85
" D. W.	12[illegible] @ [illegible]	✓	1 56
			60 14

Page 29:

Estate sale raised a total of: $575.97

Petition For Guardian Trust on Behalf of Elsie Cunningham

The image shows a handwritten legal document titled "Petition of John Cunningham for appointment of the Security Title and Trust Company as guardian of the estate of Elsie Cunningham." The document is dated February 24, 1900, and indicates that the guardian was appointed as prayed for by the court. The record is noted in Book 49, Page 302, and is signed by Allen E. Wilst, Attorney.

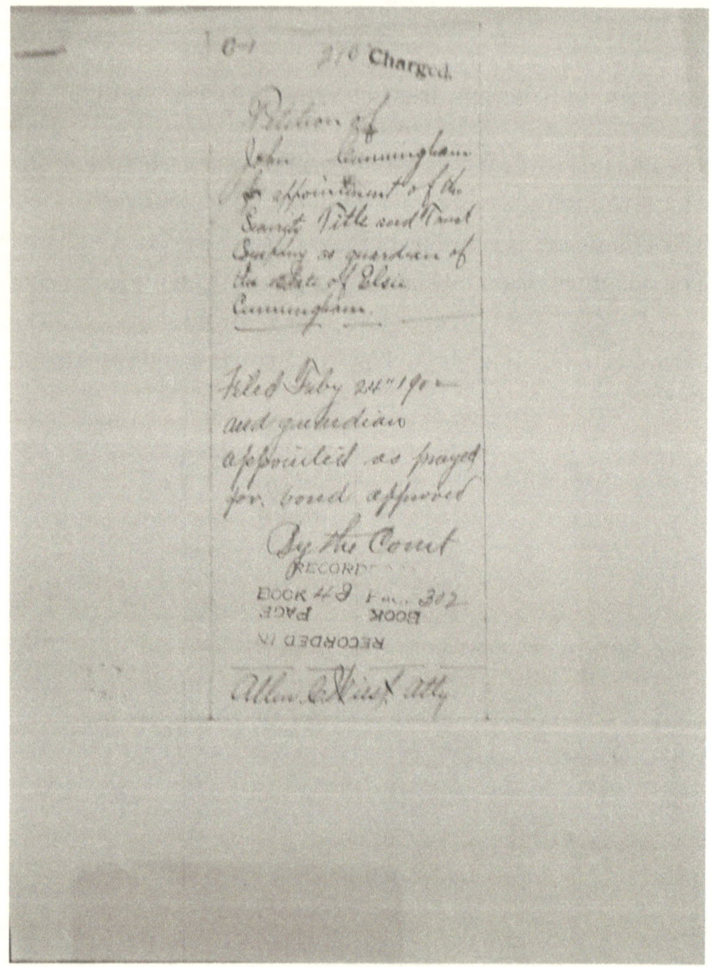

0-1 210 Charged.

Petition of
John Cunningham
for appointment of the
Security Title and Trust
Company as guardian of
the estate of Elsie
Cunningham.

Filed Feby 24" 190–
and guardian
appointed as prayed
for, bond approved
By the Court

RECORDED
BOOK 49 PAGE 302

Allen C. Wiest Atty

Page 1.

The image shows a legal document addressed to the Orphans' Court of York County, Pennsylvania. It is a petition by John Cunningham regarding the guardianship and management of a bequest left to his daughter, Elsie Cunningham, who is under the age of fourteen. The document outlines that Elsie Cunningham is to receive approximately $525.00 from the estate of William Cunningham, which is to be managed until she reaches the age of twenty-one. John Cunningham requests the court to appoint The Security Title and Trust Company of York, Pennsylvania, as the guardian of the bequest and to direct the guardian to pay the interest to him for the support of Elsie Cunningham until she reaches the age of twenty-one.

To the Orphans Court of York County, Penna.

The petition of John Cunningham respectfully represents, that he is the father of Elsie Cunningham who is under the age of fourteen years.

That under the will of William Cunningham, late of Springetsbury Township, York County, Penna., deceased, recorded in the office of Register of Wills of said County, in Will Book NN page 260, the said Elsie Cunningham will receive about $525.00, being a part of the estate of said testator, "when she becomes of age 21 years" and "until then" the said bequest "shall be put on interest, and the interest shall be paid to" your petitioner "for the support of his said daughter Elsie Cunningham"

That said Elsie Cunningham is without a guardian to care for her estate, consisting of said bequest.

Therefore your petitioner respectfully prays the Court to appoint The Security Title and Trust Company of York, Pa., guardian of the said bequest to said Elsie Cunningham, and to direct said guardian to pay to your petitioner from time to time, until said Elsie Cunningham shall reach the age of twenty one years, the income of said bequest.

J. P. Cunningham

YORK COUNTY, SS:

Personally appeared before me the undersigned, a Justice of The Peace in and for said County, who being by me duly sworn according to law, deposes and says that the facts above set forth are true, according to the best of his knowledge, information

Final page.

This document is the concluding part of a legal petition addressed to the Orphans' Court of York County, Pennsylvania. It includes the signature of John P. Cunningham and a sworn statement before a Justice of the Peace, confirming the facts presented in the petition. Additionally, it includes the signature of Elsie Cunningham, acknowledging her consent to the petition.

appoint The Security Title and Trust Company of York, Pa., guardian of the said bequest to said Elsie Cunningham, and to direct said guardian to pay to your petitioner from time to time, until said Elsie Cunningham shall reach the age of twenty one years, the income of said bequest.

J. P. Cunningham

YORK COUNTY, SS:

Personally appeared before me the undersigned, a Justice of The Peace in and for said County, who being by me duly sworn according to law, deposes and says that the facts above set forth are true, according to the best of his knowledge, information and belief.

Sworn and subscribed to before me this ....[illegible]........day of.....Feb........A.D. 1902

J. P. Cunningham

I Elsie Cunningham hereby join in the above petition

Guardian's Bond for Elsie Cunningham

The image shows a legal document titled "Guardian's Bond" from the Orphans' Court. The document is related to the guardianship of a minor child, specifically the estate of Elsie Cunningham. The bond is issued by "The Security, Title and Trust Company, of York, PA." The document is dated February 24, 1902, and is approved by the court. It is signed by an attorney and recorded in the Guardian Bond Book on page 316.

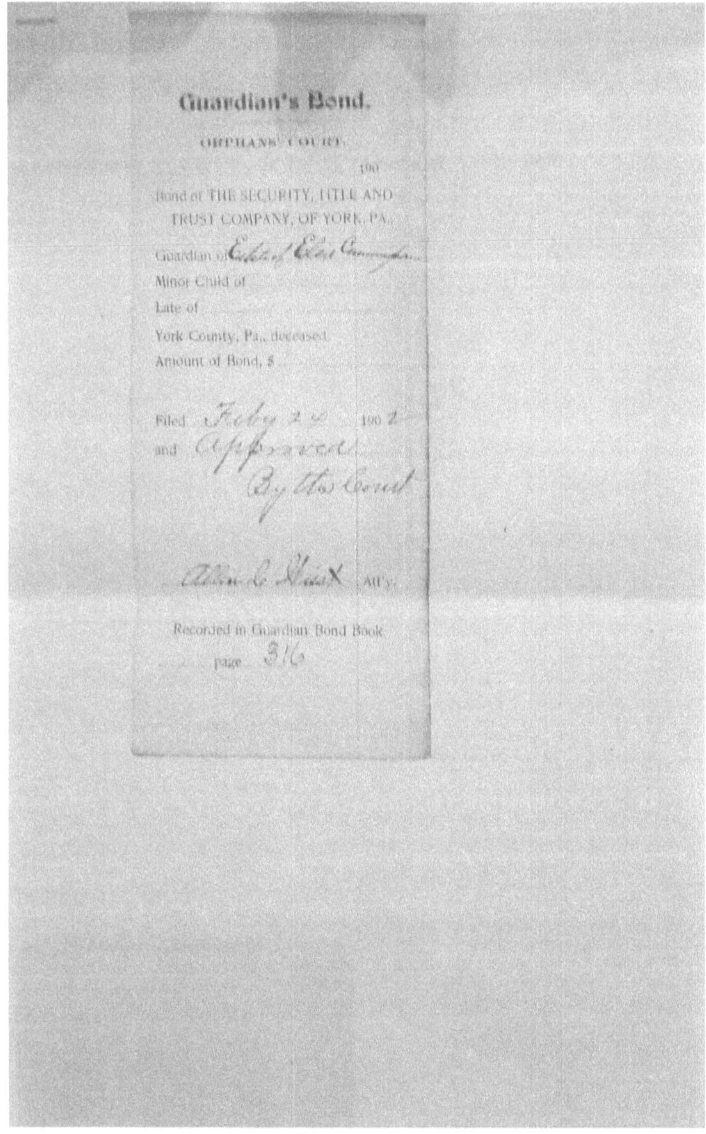

Guardian's Bond.

ORPHANS' COURT.

190

Bond of THE SECURITY, TITLE AND TRUST COMPANY, OF YORK, PA.,

Guardian of Estate of Elsie Cunningham

Minor Child of

Late of

York County, Pa., deceased.

Amount of Bond, $

Filed Feby 20 1902

and Approved

By the Court

[illegible] Att'y.

Recorded in Guardian Bond Book

page 316

The image shows a legal document titled "Know all Men by

these Presents," which appears to be a bond or obligation document from the early 1900s. It involves THE SECURITY, TITLE AND TRUST COMPANY, OF YORK, PENN'A, acting as a guardian for a minor named Elsie Cunningham. The document outlines the responsibilities of the trust company in managing the estate of the minor and ensuring proper reporting and management of the property. It is signed and sealed by the company's Vice President and Secretary.

Know all Men by these Presents,

That THE SECURITY, TITLE AND TRUST COMPANY, of YORK, PENN'A. is held and firmly bound unto the Commonwealth of Pennsylvania in the penal sum of — Ten hundred and fifty Dollars, lawful money of the United States of America, in trust for Elsie Cunningham

a minor child of —

late of — deceased, to be paid to the said Commonwealth, in trust for the use of said minor, Elsie Cunningham heirs, executors or administrators, for which payment well and truly to be made and done, the said THE SECURITY, TITLE AND TRUST COMPANY, OF YORK, PA., binds itself and its successors firmly by these presents.

Sealed with the common and corporate seal of the said THE SECURITY, TITLE AND TRUST COMPANY, OF YORK, PA., and signed by its Vice President and attested by its Secretary, and dated the 21 day of July A. D. 1902

Whereas, The said THE SECURITY, TITLE AND TRUST COMPANY, OF YORK, PA., has been appointed Guardian of the estate of the said Elsie Cunningham

by the Orphan's Court of York County, Penn'a.

Now the Condition of this Obligation is such,

THAT if the above bounden THE SECURITY, TITLE AND TRUST COMPANY, OF YORK, PA., as Guardian of the said minor, shall at least once in every three years, and at any other time when required by the Orphans' Court, for the County of York, render a just and true account of the management of the property and estate of the said minor under its care, and shall also deliver up the said property, agreeably to the Order and Decree of said Court, or the direction of law, and shall in all respects faithfully perform the duties of Guardian of said minor then the above obligation to be void and of no effect, otherwise to remain and be in full force and virtue.

H. C. Nace
Vice President.

ATTEST: A. C. Fair
Secretary.

Petition for Appointment of Trustee: Estate of William and Almeda Brown Cunningham

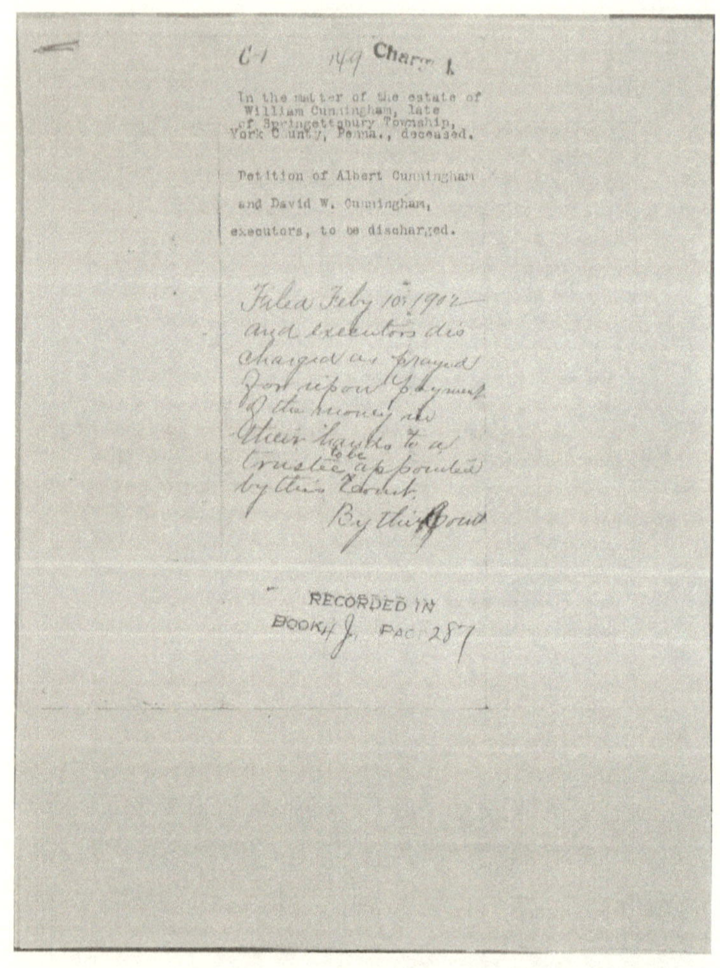

C-1 149 Charge 1

In the matter of the estate of William Cunningham, late of Springettsbury Township, York County, Penna., deceased.

Petition of Albert Cunningham and David W. Cunningham, executors, to be discharged.

Filed Feby 10th 1902 and executors discharged as prayed for upon payment of the money in their hands to a trustee to be appointed by the Court.

By the Court

RECORDED IN BOOK 4 J. PAG 287

This document is a typed legal petition addressed to the Judges of the Orphans' Court of York County, Pennsylvania. The petition is from Albert Cunningham and David W. Cunningham, executors of the last will and testament of William Cunningham, deceased. The document outlines the provisions of William Cunningham's will, specifically regarding the inheritance of his son, William Cunningham, and his first wife, Almeda Cunningham. The petitioners request the court to discharge them as trustees of the fund and appoint a competent person or persons in their place.

Transcription of the document:

To the Honorable, the Judges of the Orphans' Court of York County, Penna.

The petition of Albert Cunningham and David W. Cunningham respectfully represents:— That they are the executors of the last
will and testament of William Cunningham, late of Springettsbury
Township, in said County, deceased.

That in his last will and testament, which was duly admitted
to probate by the Register of Wills of said County, on July 28, 1899,
and remaining on file in his office, and is recorded in Will Book
"2-J", No. 214, page 266, the said testator provided, inter

alia, as follows:—

"The share coming to my son, William Cunningham, I bequeath one half to his first wife, Almeda Cunningham, nee Brown, she to have the interest of it only so long as she lives, after her death it shall go to her son, Henry (sic Harry) Cunningham, the other half shall go to my son, William Cunningham."

That your petitioners have filed their final account as executors of said will, that said account has been finally confirmed, and that an Auditor has been appointed to distribute the balance thereon.

That your petitioners are not willing to assume the duty of holding the half of the share of William Cunningham and investing the same during the life of the said Almeda Cunningham, and paying to her during her life.

They therefore pray your Honorable Court, to discharge them, as Trustees of said fund, and to appoint some competent person, or persons, as trustees, in their place and stead. And they will ever pray, etc.

Albert Cunningham

David W. Cunningham

To the Honorable, the Judges of the Orphans' Court of York County, Penna.

The petition of Albert Cunningham and David W. Cunningham respectfully represents:-- That they are the executors of the last will and testament of William Cunningham, late of Springettsbury Township, in said County, deceased.

That in his last will and testament, which was duly admitted to probate by the Register of Wills of said County, on July 28, 1899, and remaining on file in his office, and is recorded in Will Book " 2-H", No. 214, page 266, the said testator provided, inter alia, as follows:--

"The share coming to my son, William Cunningham, I bequeath one half to his first wife, Almeda Cunningham, nee Brown, she to have the interest of it only so long as she lives, after her death it shall go to her son, Henry Cunningham, the other half shall go to my son, William Cunningham."

That your petitioners have filed their final account as executors of said will, that said account has been finally confirmed, and that an Auditor has been appointed to distribute the balance thereon.

That your petitioners are not willing to assume the duty of holding the half of the share of William Cunningham and investing the same during the life of the said Almeda Cunningham, and paying to her during her life.

They therefore pray your Honorable Court, to discharge them, as Trustees of said fund, and to appoint some competent person, or persons, as trustee, in their place and stead. And they will ever pray, etc.

Albert Cunningham
David W. Cunningham

This document is the concluding part of a legal petition addressed to the Judges of the Orphans' Court of York County,

Pennsylvania. It contains an affirmation by David W. Cunningham and Albert Cunningham, stating that the facts set forth in the petition are true to the best of their knowledge and belief. The document is signed by both individuals and a notary public named A. N. Green.

York County, ss:

David W. Cunningham and Albert Cunningham, being duly affirmed according to law, did depose and say, that the facts set forth in the within petition are true, to the best of their knowledge and belief.

Affirmed and subscribed before me this fifth day of February, 1902.

Albert Cunningham
David W. Cunningham

A. A. Green
Notary Public.
My Commission Expires Jan. 18, 1903.

Trustee Granted: Estate of William and Almeda Brown Cunningham

The image shows a legal document related to the estate of William Cunningham, late of Springettsbury Township, York County, Pennsylvania. The document is a petition by Almeda Cunningham for the appointment of a trustee. The handwritten portion indicates that the petition was filed on March 10, 1902, and that the trustee appointment was approved by the court. The document is recorded in Book 49, Page 345.

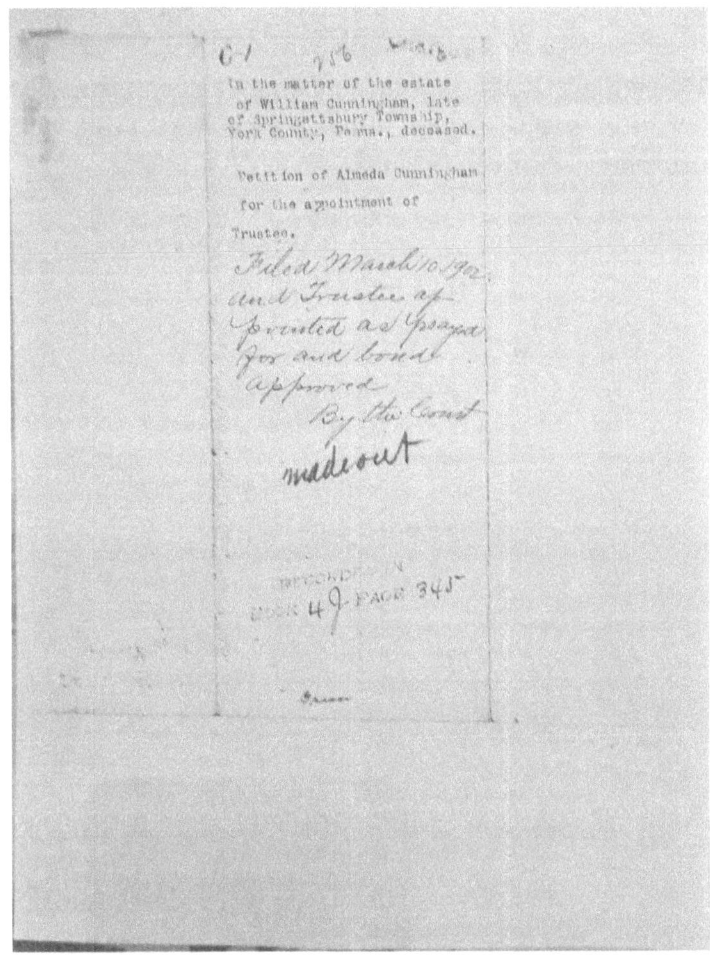
In the matter of the estate of William Cunningham, late of Springettsbury Township, York County, Penna., deceased.

Petition of Almeda Cunningham for the appointment of Trustee.

Filed March 10 1902 and Trustee appointed as prayed for and bond approved By the Court

made out

RECORDED IN BOOK 49 PAGE 345

The document is a typed legal petition addressed to the Judges of the Orphans' Court of York County, Pennsylvania. The petition is from Almeda Cunningham, requesting the appointment of the York Trust Company as trustee for the fund mentioned in the will of William Cunningham. The petition outlines the provisions of William Cunningham's will, particularly the share intended for his son, William Cunningham, and the interest to be received by Almeda Cunningham during her lifetime. The petitioners, Almeda Cunningham and Henry (misspelled Harry) Cunningham, request the court to appoint the York Trust Company as the trustee of the said fund.

To the Honorable, the Judges of the Orphans' Court of York County, Penna.

The petition of Almeda Cunningham respectfully represents:-- That in and by the last will and testament, admitted to probate by the Register of Wills of said County, on the 28th day of July, 1899, remaining on file in his office, and recorded in Will Book, "2-H", No. 314, page 236, William Cunningham, late of Springettsbury Township, provided, inter alia, as follows:--

"The share coming to my son, William Cunningham, I bequeath one half to his first wife, Almeda Cunningham, nee Brown, she to have the interest of it only so long as she lives, after her death it shall go to her son, Henry Cunningham, the other half shall go to my son, William Cunningham."

That your petitioners are, respectively, Almeda Cunningham and Henry Cunningham, named in the above-recited portion of the will of the said William Cunningham.

That the executors of said William Cunningham have filed their final account, asexecutors, and an Auditor has been appointed to make distribution of the balance thereon.

That said executors have declined to act as trustee of the portion of the share of said William Cunningham, upon which the said Almeda Cunningham is entitled to receive the interest during her life.

Your petitioners therefore pray your Honorable Court to appoint The York Trust Company, Trustee of said fund, under the above recited portion of said will. And they will ever pray, etc.

Witness John H. Brown

Almeda Cunningham

Harry B. Cunningham

Affirmed and Subscribed before me this 12. day of Feby 1902

My Commission Expires FEB. 27th, 1905.

This document is the concluding part of a legal petition addressed to the Judges of the Orphans' Court of York County, Pennsylvania. It includes an affirmation by Henry (Harry) B. Cunningham, stating that the facts set forth in the petition are true to the best of his knowledge and belief. The document is signed by Harry B. Cunningham and a notary public named A. N. Green.

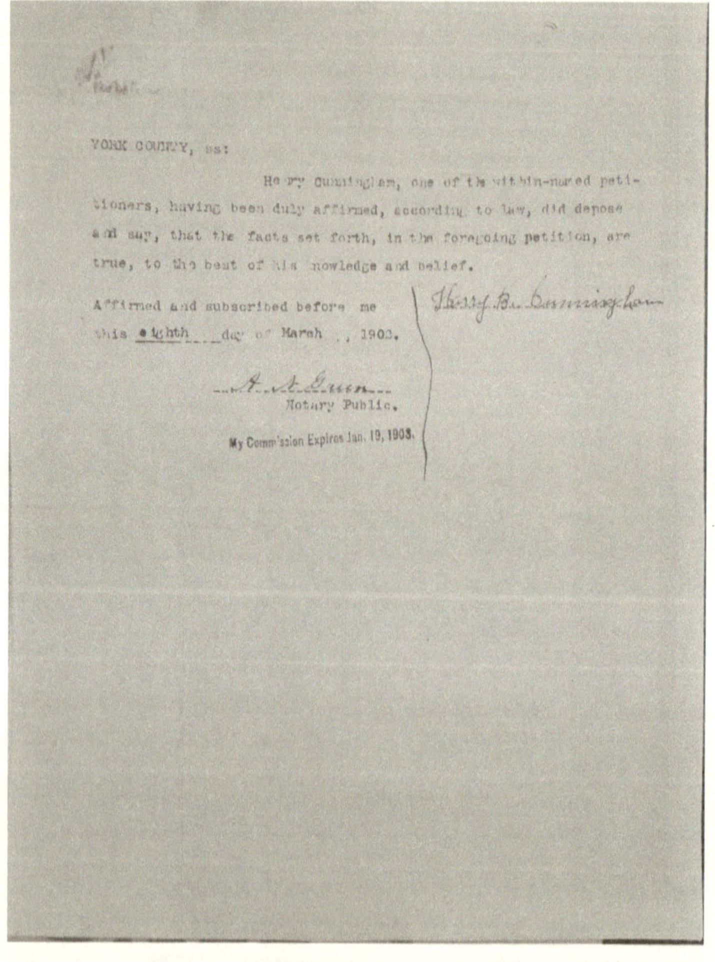

YORK COUNTY, ss:

Henry Cunningham, one of the within-named petitioners, having been duly affirmed, according to law, did depose and say, that the facts set forth, in the foregoing petition, are true, to the best of his knowledge and belief.

Affirmed and subscribed before me this eighth day of March, 1902.

Harry B. Cunningham

A. N. Green
Notary Public.

My Commission Expires Jan. 19, 1903.

This page concludes the legal petition involving Almeda Brown Cunningham and her son, Harry (incorrectly typed as Henry)

Cunningham. It includes affirmations by Albert Cunningham and David W. Cunningham, confirming that the facts set forth in the petition are true. Additionally, it contains Almeda Cunningham's acknowledgment and request for the petition to be recorded.

Albert Cunningham and David W. Cunningham, the within-named petitioners, having been duly affirmed according to law, did depose and say, that the facts set forth, in the foregoing petition, are true, to the best of their knowledge and belief.

Albert Cunningham
David W. Cunningham

Affirmed and subscribed before me this 12th day of February, 1902.

[illegible]
Notary Public.

State of Pennsylvania } SS
County of Lancaster }

Personally appeared before me a Notary Public in and for the County and State aforesaid affirmed and signed the Petition aforesaid one Almeda Cunningham and in due form of law acknowledges it to be her act & deed and desires that it may be recorded as such and deposes and says that the facts set forth in the foregoing petition are true.

Given under my hand and Notarial Seal this 12th day of February 1902

[illegible]
Notary Public

My Commission Expires
FEB. 27th. 1905

Trustee Bond: Estate of William and Almeda Brown Cunningham

The image shows a legal document with handwritten text indicating the approval of a petition related to the estate of William Cunningham. The document confirms the appointment of a trustee for Almeda Brown Cunningham as prayed for in the petition. It includes a note that the petition was filed on March 10, 1902, and was approved by the court. The document is recorded in Book 4, Page 346.

Filed March 10 1902
and approved
By the Court

This legal document is a bond from the York Trust Company, dated March 8, 1902, and it outlines the conditions under which the company is appointed as the trustee of a fund bequeathed by William Cunningham. The bond amount is $520.00, and it ensures that the York Trust Company will faithfully execute its duties as trustee, managing the fund for the benefit of Almeda Cunningham during her lifetime and subsequently for her son, Harry Cunningham (incorrectly typed as Henry in previous documents).

KNOW ALL MEN BY THESE PRESENTS, that York Trust Company, of York, Penna., a corporation duly organized under the laws of the State of Pennsylvania, is held and firmly bound unto the Commonwealth of Pennsylvania, in the sum of Five Hundred and Twenty ($520.00) Dollars, lawful money of the United States, to be paid to the said Commonwealth in trust for all persons interested in the fund hereinafter referred to, to which payment well and truly to be made, the said York Trust Company doth hereby bind itself, its successors and assigns, firmly by these presents.

Sealed with the common and corporate seal of the said York Trust Company, and duly attested by its President and Secretary, this eighth day of March, one thousand nine hundred and two.

WHEREAS, the said York Trust Company is about to be appointed by the Orphans Court of York County, Trustee of the fund bequeathed by William Cunningham, late of Springettsbury Township, in said County, deceased, to Almeda Cunningham, nee Brown, first wife of William Cunningham, the son of said testator; she to have the interest of it only so long as she lives, after her death it shall go to her son, Henry Cunningham; as by reference to the will of said William Cunningham, duly admitted to probate by the Register of Wills of said County, on the 22nd day of July, 1899, remaining on file in his office and recorded in Will Book "2-N", No. 214, page 266, and to the petition upon which said appointment was made, filed in the office of the Clerk of said Orphans' Court, will fully appear.

Now the condition of this obligation is such, that if the above bounden York Trust Company, Trustee as aforesaid, shall faithfully execute the said trust, and perform the duties of its appointment according to law, and as provided in the above in part recited portion of the last will and testament of said William Cunningham, deceased, then this obligation to be void, otherwise to be and remain in full force and virtue.

Sealed and delivered in the Presence of:

York Trust Company

By [illegible] President

[illegible] Secretary

Guardian's Bond: Zachariah Myers

The image shows a legal document titled "Guardian's Bond" from the Orphans' Court. The document pertains to the guardianship of Zachariah Myers, a minor child of Ellen (Cunningham) Myers and Horace D. Myers, both deceased and grandson of William Cunningham, late of Springettsbury Township. The bond is issued by George E. Loucks, who is named as the guardian. The document includes the amount of the bond, which is $200.00, and it is approved by the court on March 20, 1902. The document is recorded in the Guardian Bond Book H, page 103.

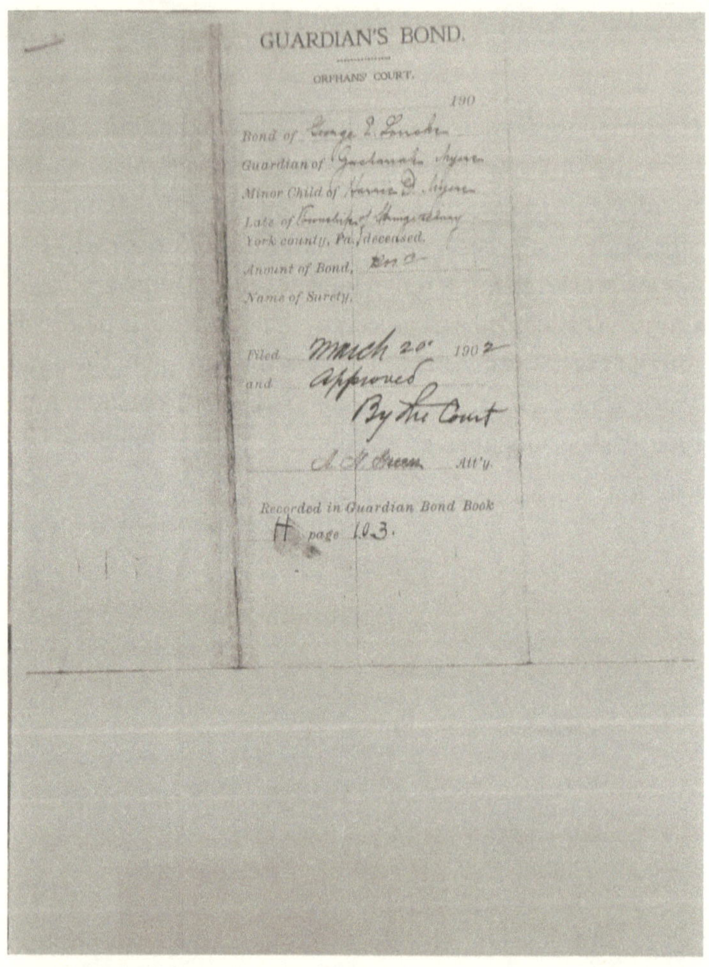

GUARDIAN'S BOND.

ORPHANS' COURT.

190

Bond of George E. Loucks

Guardian of Zachariah Myers

Minor Child of [illegible] Myers

Late of Township of [illegible]

York county, Pa., deceased.

Amount of Bond, [illegible]

Name of Surety,

Filed March 20 1902
and Approved
By the Court

[illegible] Att'y.

Recorded in Guardian Bond Book
H page 103.

This document is the concluding part of a legal bond agreement involving George E. Loucks and Alexander W. Loucks as guardians of Zachariah Myers. It outlines the bond conditions to ensure proper management of the minor's estate and property, including rendering accounts to the Orphans' Court of York County, Pennsylvania, as required. The document includes the signatures of the guardians and witnesses.

Know all Men by these Presents,

That George E. Loucks [illegible]

are held and firmly bound unto the Commonwealth of Pennsylvania, in the sum of [illegible] Dollars, lawful money of the said Commonwealth in trust for [illegible] Myers [illegible] minor son of [illegible] Myers [illegible] late of the [illegible] of [illegible] deceased, to be paid to the said Commonwealth in trust for the use of said minor, [illegible] heirs, executors or administrators, for which payment well and truly to be made and done, we bind ourselves jointly and severally, our and each of our heirs, executors and administrators, firmly by these presents.

Sealed with our seals, dated the [illegible] day of March in the year of our Lord one thousand nine hundred and [illegible]

WHEREAS, the above named George E. Loucks on the [illegible] day of March having been appointed Guardian of the person and estate of the said [illegible] Myers by the Orphans' Court of the said County of York.

Now the Conditions of this Obligation is such,

That if the above bounden George E. Loucks Guardian of the said [illegible] Myers shall at least once in every three years, and at any other time when required by the Orphans' Court, for the County of York, render a just and true account of the management of the property and estate of the said minor under [illegible] care, and shall also deliver up the said property, agreeably to the Order and Decree of said Court, or the direction of law, and shall in all respects faithfully perform the duties of Guardian of said [illegible] Myers

then the above obligation to be void and of no effect, otherwise to remain and be in full force and virtue.

Sealed and delivered in the presence of

Eli S. Brohtel — George E. Loucks (SEAL)

[illegible] — Alexander W. Loucks (SEAL)

(SEAL)

Guardian's Bond for Annie Minerva Myers

The image shows a Guardian's Bond document from the Orphans' Court dated 1902. This document is for George E. Loucks, who is the guardian of Annie Minerva Myers, a minor child of Ellen (Cunningham) and Horace D. Myers (sic Harris), late of York County, Pennsylvania, both deceased and the granddaughter of William Cunningham, late of Springettsbury Township. The bond amount is $200. The document was filed and approved on April 1st, 1902, and recorded in Guardian Bond Book 16, page 104.

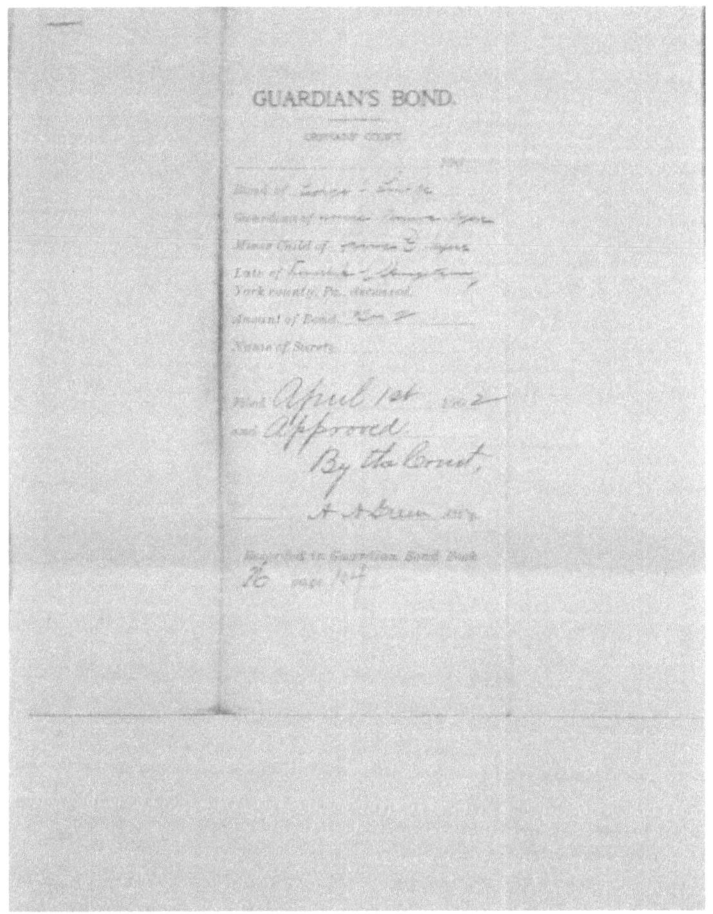

GUARDIAN'S BOND.

Bond of

Guardians of

Minor Child of

Late of

York county, Pa., deceased.

Amount of Bond

Names of Sureties

Filed April 1st 1902

and Approved

By the Court,

A. A. Green

Recorded in Guardian Bond Book

76 page

This page concludes the legal bond agreement involving George E. Loucks and Alexander W. Loucks as guardians of Annie Minerva Myers. It outlines the bond conditions to ensure proper management of the minor's estate and property, including rendering accounts to the Orphans' Court of York County, Pennsylvania, as required. The document is dated the twelfth day of March in the year 1902 and includes signatures of the involved parties and witnesses.

Know all Men by these Presents,

That George E. Loucks of

Are held and firmly bound unto the Commonwealth of Pennsylvania, in the sum of Dollars, lawful money of the said Commonwealth in trust for minor late of the of deceased, to be paid to the said Commonwealth in trust for the use of said minor, her heirs, executors or administrators, for which payment well and truly to be made and done, we bind ourselves jointly and severally, our and each of our heirs, executors and administrators, firmly by these presents.

Sealed with our seals, dated the day of in the year of our Lord one thousand nine hundred and two.

WHEREAS, the above named on the day of having been appointed Guardian of the person and estate of the said by the Orphans' Court of the said County of York.

Now the Conditions of this Obligation is such,

That if the above bounden Guardian of the said shall at least once in every three years, and at any other time when required by the Orphans' Court, for the County of York, render a just and true account of the management of the property and estate of the said minor under his care, and shall also deliver up the said property, agreeably to the Order and Decree of said Court, or the direction of law, and shall in all respects faithfully perform the duties of Guardian of said

Then the above obligation to be void and of no effect, otherwise to remain and be in full force and virtue.

Sealed and delivered in the presence of

SEAL

SEAL

SEAL

Guardian's Bond: Wilbur H. Myers

The image shows a Guardian's Bond document from the Orphans' Court, dated 1902. This document is for George E. Loucks, who is the guardian of Wilbur H. Myers, a minor child of Horace D. Myers (sic Harris) and Ellen Cunningham Myers, both deceased and grandchild of William Cunningham, late of Springettsbury Township. The bond amount is $200. The document was filed and approved on March 20th, 1902, and recorded in Guardian Bond Book H, page 167.

GUARDIAN'S BOND.

ORPHANS' COURT

190

Bond of [illegible]

Guardian of [illegible]

Minor Child of [illegible]

Late of [illegible]
York county, Pa., deceased.

Amount of Bond, [illegible]

Name of Surety,

Filed March 20" 1902
and Approved
By the Court,

[illegible] Att'y.

Recorded in Guardian Bond Book
H page 62

This page concludes the legal bond agreement involving George E. Loucks and Alexander W. Loucks as guardians of Wilbur H. Myers. It outlines the bond conditions to ensure proper management of the minor's estate and property, including rendering accounts to the Orphans' Court of York County, Pennsylvania, as required. The document is dated the twelfth day of March in the year 1902 and includes signatures of the involved parties and witnesses.

That George E. Loucks and Alexander W. Loucks of York County Pennsylvania

Are held and firmly bound unto the Commonwealth of Pennsylvania in the sum of Five Hundred ($500) Dollars,

lawful money of the said Commonwealth in trust for William H. Myers minor son of [illegible] Myers, [illegible]

late of the Township of [illegible] deceased, to be paid to the said Commonwealth in trust for the use of said minor, his heirs, executors or administrators, for which payment well and truly to be made and done, we bind ourselves jointly and severally, our and each of our heirs, executors and administrators, firmly by these presents.

Sealed with our seals, dated the twelfth day of March in the year of our Lord one thousand nine hundred and two

WHEREAS, the above named George E. Loucks on the day of March having been appointed Guardian of the person and estate of the said William H. Myers by the Orphans' Court of the said County of York.

Now the Conditions of this Obligation is such,

That if the above bounden George E. Loucks Guardian of the said William H. Myers shall at least once in every three years, and at any other time when required by the Orphans' Court, for the County of York, render a just and true account of the management of the property and estate of the said minor under care, and shall also deliver up the said property, agreeably to the Order and Decree of said Court, or the direction of law, and shall in all respects faithfully perform the duties of Guardian of said William H. Myers

then the above obligation to be void and of no effect, otherwise to remain and be in full force and virtue.

Sealed and delivered in the presence of

Eli L. Bechtel

[illegible]

George E. Loucks (SEAL)

Alexander W. Loucks. (SEAL)

(SEAL)

7

Acknowledgements and References

I began my genealogy project on the Cunningham family of York County, Pennsylvania, in 1998. At that time, I only had a few names and the knowledge that my third great-grandfather was a county commissioner. With limited internet access, I turned to online genealogy message boards.

Fortunately, I connected with a gentleman named Walter Keesy from Red Lion, Pennsylvania. He generously offered to assist me with my research, as he frequently visited local libraries and historical societies in York. His efforts were invaluable, providing me with a wealth of family history and names related to the county commissioner. This gave me a solid foundation to build upon. I will forever be grateful for his help.

Much of the information he provided came from George Prowell's History of York County, Pennsylvania.

With a good collection of family history, I decided to visit York and conduct extensive research at the libraries and historical society. I was joined by my mother, Nelda Mae Cunningham, the great-great-granddaughter of William Cunningham, the former county commissioner.

We spent countless hours poring over microfilm of newspaper clippings, census records, death records, and marriage certificates, taking notes of anything related to our family. We also visited the Mt. Zion Lutheran Church and Cemetery in Springettsbury Township, Pennsylvania, to search for family connections and take photos. This trip yielded valuable information that allowed us to begin creating a family tree and connecting the family members.

I extend my sincere gratitude to my beloved mother for her countless hours of note-taking, information gathering, and typing.

A project of this magnitude requires information from various sources to confirm historical facts and ensure the accuracy of dates, names, and marriages.

Many individuals, both within and outside my family, contributed to this project. Without their help, this book would not have been possible. I would like to acknowledge the following:

- **Stephen H. Smith:** A renowned author from York, Pennsylvania, who generously shared his meticulous research on census data, property records, and other sources. His work definitively confirmed the family homestead of John Cunningham, which is depicted on the book cover.
- **Roy Brown Cunningham:** Son of Harry Brown Cunningham, Jr., for his research and contributions to the family history.
- **Doris Louise Cunningham:** Daughter of Harry Brown Cunningham, Jr., for her recollections of family history

and the contributions of her late husband Arthur Smith and daughter Karen Christner.

- **Denise Hennessey and Tammy Sebek:** Granddaughters of Harry Brown Cunningham, Sr., and Mary (McGinnis) Cunningham, for their research and contributions.

If I have inadvertently omitted anyone who contributed, I apologize.

I hope that everyone who reads this book enjoys the efforts of many in providing a historical glimpse into the Cunningham family of York County, Pennsylvania.

Warm regards,

Ronald Matheny

www.ingramcontent.com/pod-product-compliance
Lightning Source LLC
Chambersburg PA
CBHW021158160726
47994CB00001B/271

* 9 7 9 8 2 3 0 2 4 9 0 3 0 *